THE NEXT MARKETING

TO HEALTHCARE PROFESSIONALS

HARSHIT JAIN MD

Copyright © Harshit Jain MD, 2022

The right of Harshit Jain MD to be identified as the author of this work has been asserted in accordance with the Copyright, Design and Patents Act, 1988

The scanning, uploading, and distribution of this book without permission is a theft of the author's intellectual property.
If you would like permission to use material from the book (other than for review purposes), please contact
info@thenextmarketing.us
Thank you for your support of the author's rights.

Paper back : 979-8-9868961-0-6
e-book : 979-8-9868961-1-3

@doctorhj
First Edition: September 2022

Fortunate are those who come across mentors who believe in them, having deep faith in their commitment to make a difference.

I am indebted to my mentor and my guide without whose support I wouldn't have been where I am today.

With a lot of gratitude, I humbly dedicate this book to the notable writer, poet, lyricist and globally-acclaimed communication specialist, marketer and advertising veteran, **Prasoon Joshi**.

'It's not an experiment if you know it's going to work'

Jeff Bezos

Contents

Preface

Introduction

01	What is Point-of-Care Messaging	003
02	The Evolution of Point-of-Care Messaging	017
03	Types of Point-of-Care Messaging	031
04	The HCP-Patient Relationship at the Point-of- Care	043
05	The Advancement of Measurement Technologies for Impactful Messaging	051
06	Point-of-Care Messaging Myths	067
07	Adhere to Industry Regulations for Point-of-Care Messaging	075
08	A Global Perspective on the Point-of-Care Messaging Landscape	081
09	What Life Sciences Brands Need to Know About HCP Communications	089
10	Understanding the Digital Workflow of HCPs	101
11	Telehealth – The New Point-of-Care	111
12	EHR & EHR Apps – Communications During an HCP's Workflow	123

13	eRx Transforms Digital Communications	137
14	Providing Patient Assistance During Point-of-Care Messaging Campaigns	145
15	Technologies to Advance Point-of-Care Communications	155
16	Identifying the Right Approach for a Messaging Campaign	165
17	How Does Point-of-Care Messaging Help	171
18	An Assessment of the Point-of-Care Messaging Landscape	179
19	The Decision to Introduce Ad Slots Within a Point-of-Care Platform	185
20	Messaging Formats to Facilitate Point-of-Care Campaigns to HCPs	191
21	Advance the Deployment of Telehealth Offerings	197
22	EHR & EHR Apps Foster New Messaging Offerings During an HCP's Journey	203
23	Elevate eRx Point-of-Care Messaging Offerings	209
24	Optimize Inventory Offerings to Boost Revenue	215
	References	221
	List of Figures	226

Preface

Communicating with healthcare professionals (HCPs) at the point-of-care (POC) can be a great support to clinicians as they tend to their patients, enabling them to deliver better care. When I was a practicing physician of internal medicine, I experienced the value of marketing programs being distributed to prescribers. So, I wanted to share my expertise on the current state of messaging within online POC platforms s to provide a resource that will elevate the way digital channels are being utilized for communication initiatives in the life sciences sector.

The Covid-19 pandemic accelerated the use of virtual platforms in the life sciences industry to facilitate messaging campaigns to providers. I want to strengthen the efficiency and effectiveness of digital messaging strategies to transform the category. With my book, I intend to raise the education of marketers and platforms on all facets of POC communications to let them thrive as the digital messaging landscape evolves for the industry.

After I stopped practicing medicine, I worked at a leadership position at McCann Health for global marketing programs and later developed a global platform for HCP programmatic messaging with proprietary solutions as the founder of Doceree. I thus intend to support organizations in improving communications that are conducted within the virtual settings to enable them to seamlessly adapt to digital practices for achieving desired outcomes. With my knowledge of medicine and experience in the advertising sector, I want my book to be a guide for brands, agencies, platforms and healthcare information technology (HIT) sites. It intends to elevate the POC messaging campaigns that are created and distributed to clinicians.

While the history of in-person marketing efforts to reach prescribers has been well documented, the ventures and tactics of online POC messaging have not been. I'll provide essential learnings throughout the book to assist organizations in enriching the messaging practices and platform offerings in this sector that are crucial to navigate the digital ecosystem at the POC.

Introduction

Interactions with HCPs at the point-of-care (POC) was once limited to the clinician's office. Those instances consistently lacked personalization as I recognized countless physicians in my medical field receiving the same branded brochures, posters, and additional marketing materials.

The Covid-19 pandemic led to an acceleration of digital communications in the life sciences industry that has altered the POC ecosystem. Consequently, a comprehensive understanding of the POC category is pivotal to improve the care patients get. As POC channels are a part of a clinician's online journey, I'll signify the essential messaging practices and offerings to reach providers within online mediums.

Marketers can improve an individual's health by delivering relevant information at opportune moments, prompting a provider to make an accurate diagnosis or proceed with a therapy that leads a person to fully recover from their ailments. Brands that understand a physician's specialty can offer educational resources to prescribers to expand their awareness of new medical developments that enrich a patient's experience during their medical visit.

The ability to target prescribers accurately to distribute a personalized message during their workflow provides enormous potential to advance the POC ecosystem. The burgeoning market of POC platforms can help strengthen the HCP-patient relationship in the evolving virtual communications settings.

With the capacity to decipher the impact of POC messaging strategies and offerings, marketers and platforms can better comprehend digital interactions that are being held to successfully navigate POC networks for establishing meaningful communication with HCPs.

In this book, I'll delve into POC best practices, learnings, advancements, and tactics to lay a foundation of meaningful communication campaigns and offerings, cultivating a digital environment that supports HCPs to achieve optimal health outcomes for their patients.

WHAT IS POINT-OF-CARE MESSAGING?

Digital communications have undoubtedly progressed for the life sciences industry. From walking the halls of Northwestern Memorial Hospital to being at the forefront of the virtual era of medical marketing by developing a platform designed for marketers to reach HCPs, the category has undergone a transformation in the way online messages are delivered to physicians at the point-of-care (POC).

Messaging at the POC is when brand communications are being delivered to either an HCP or patient during the healthcare journey of the physician and their patients. The point-of-care communications take place across a multitude of channels, including telehealth, e-prescribing (eRx), electronic health record (EHR) and EHR apps.

The potential of the space is exemplified with the ad spending in the category. Overall, digital ad spending in the United Stated reached $191.09 billion in 2021, an increase of 25.5% compared to 2020.[1] The usage of digital channels also grew massively within the healthcare and pharma industry with the category seeing an ad spending of up to $11.25 billion.[2] Further, the business-to-business digital healthcare and pharma ad spending exceeded $1 billion for the first time in 2021.[3]

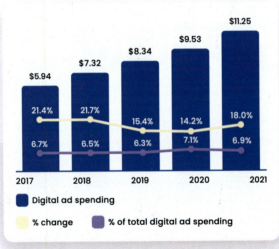

Fig 1:

Healthcare & Pharma Industry Digital Ad Spending in the US, 2017-2021

Drawing a parallel: Communications in the life sciences and consumer space

POC messaging in the life sciences industry is similar to what consumer marketers have been practicing.

As I reflect on the premise of POC messaging, the objectives for life sciences organizations to connect with HCPs mirror the efforts of consumer marketing companies implementing strategies to reach their target audience. With consumer-specific initiatives, marketers craft campaigns to influence the purchasing decisions of their target audience during their online presence.

As a brand identifies its target audience, a business begins pursuing them with communications within cyber channels as they are navigating online platforms during their daily activities. When consumers are the focal point of a marketing program, the messages are measured via the sales that are derived from the communications. Across the digital ecosystem, marketers interact with consumers until the individual reaches the point of purchase. So, corporations set a point-of-sale marketing approach to have various touchpoints with an individual on their path to purchase.

For instance, a shopper that visits Amazon or any other online retailer to browse for a new television is a high target for a consumer electronic brand that manufactures the one in which the individual displayed interest. Upon exiting the website without making a purchase, the consumer is then strategically targeted by the brand to re-engage the person with the item. Serving personalized messages to consumers that reflect their interest raises the probability that the individual will click on the content to absorb the complete message.

> **Formulate messages to coincide with the buyer's journey that aligns with their needs.**

In addition, when a product is added into the cart of a buyer, but removed later, this presents an opportunity to swiftly regain consideration from an individual to maintain the relevance of proceeding with a purchase. A individual's schedule is busy and brands stand the possibility of being forgotten amid the noise across digital channels. Thus, the delivery of timely and relevant content enhances the recognition of a brand following those moments when a customer appeared disengaged with the procurement of a product. With personalized communications along their digital journey, the decisiveness of an individual can be influenced to proceed with a purchase.

The moments to target a shopper with a message are instrumental in the success of a marketing campaign. If the person is browsing an online news outlet without having viewed an add for an item first, then the significance of a message appearing on their screen may not reflect the consumer's buying interests. However, when a coupon is served to a person in the process of deciding, then the content being received is tailored to an item that appeals to them and can incentivize the buyer to proceed with the purchase of the item. Sales are achieved by reaching people at decision-making moments, and a comprehensive communication plan needs to be in place to close in on a buyer. In the absence of strategic messaging, the individual's purchasing choices will be unclear and an opportunity to engage a person will be lost.

Therefore, data analytics have a key role to identify the moments, channels, formats, and the type of content that garner the highest success rate for marketing campaigns within POC platforms.

When seeking an understanding of a physician's workflow, the metrics for messages across the digital networks enable marketers to capture moments that are most influential to interact with an HCP. Further, intel on a clinician's communication preferences within POC channels creates a positive atmosphere for messaging efforts. Also, data points such as the physician's prescribing behaviors empower marketers to gain momentum throughout the online systems to connect with providers. Besides, marketers learn which messages are effective, and can accordingly identify a mixture of communications across POC channels that will result in a prescription being written by the targeted HCP.

> Embrace data analytics to understand the optimal path to reach HCPs.

A physician's workflow across digital mediums encompasses a similar path as that of a consumer. Marketers establish connections that result in their business objectives being met. The jam-packed schedules that HCPs must manage leave them with little time to explore educational materials for their patients that can aid their diagnosis. The usage of POC platforms is so prevalent that physician burnout is experienced at times.

In fact, of the **37%** of physicians that indicated one or more symptoms of burnout in a study,[4] **75%** of them attributed it to the use of EHR systems.[5]

Brands can streamline the access to valuable resources to better support prescribers within the virtual mediums.

When the messages deliver required information to the HCPs, they don't have to spend time on gathering supportive materials to tend to their patient. After all, 95% of physicians that spent more than six hours weekly after work on an EHR were nearly four times likely to attribute their burnout to the platform.[6]

With the widespread use of EHR systems by providers during most of their work hours, life sciences corporations want to be in front of physicians throughout their workflow. Brands interact with HCPs through their sales representatives in their office settings. Now, this engagement also happens within the digital landscape of point-of-care networks. As providers are caring for their patients, communications that demonstrate value in improving an individual's health outcomes are going to create more awareness for a company. During virtual care, marketers can reach physicians within POC channels to advance their knowledge while they are in the medical mindset. By addressing the pain points of providers with pertinent communications, the fluid exchanges will provide information that will build a higher level of trust for the brand with their target audience.

Marketers need to plan for messages in such a way that they don't disrupt the digital workflow of the clinicians and can proceed to care for their patients without interruption. Life sciences brands must reach HCPs during their online journey with patients to gain their attention with a message. While, a consumer-driven message may be showcasing the latest smartphone, communications that a provider receives must focus on areas within their specialty such as a new drug entering the market, research about a therapy or symptoms of a disease to support the care afforded to an individual. It intends to strengthen the physician-patient relationship with respect to the exchanges taking place within virtual point-of-care networks.

While in-office visits were once the predominant form for healthcare interactions, online platforms have expanded the avenues for patients to consult physicians with the utilization of telehealth platforms at **38 times higher than prior to the Covid-19 pandemic**.[7] POC messaging at a physician's office earlier covered materials that were prominently displayed at the facility, such as posters on the walls, brochures dispersed across a table or medical videos being played. The momentum of POC messaging has gone beyond the interior walls of a doctor's office to the online ecosystem that has progressed the messaging capabilities of life sciences brands to expand their communications repertoire and proceed digitally to reach HCPs while providing virtual care to their patients.

Point-of-care messaging: Patient versus HCP

For the market, POC messaging falls under two types of target audiences — patient and HCP. When developing a POC communication strategy, understanding which type of audience the campaign is targeting is essential. While marketing in waiting rooms and a physician's examination rooms still offers value to organizations to generate awareness with caregivers, for this book, my focus will be on digital messaging strategies and the elevation of communications with prescribers within POC platforms. The understanding of the HCP and patient activities and preferences offers an opportunity for digital communications to be elevated within the online platforms to better support the intended audience.

An HCP has an array of responsibilities in the medical field. So, grasping their professional duties at the POC affords marketers to better communicate with their target audience. Thus, HCPs need to receive messages in a manner that illustrates the value it will provide them in fulfilling their professional obligations.

Clinicians, such as physicians and nurses, that have the medical knowledge base to instruct the delivery of care to patients have a direct line to individuals. This is a group that is the primary focus during digital POC efforts with the uninterrupted path from consultation to a prescription being written.

This leads to the prescribing stage of an EHR network or the utilization of an eRx platform where messages can be shared with a pharmacist. Therefore, communications during a pharmacist's workflow serve as a resource of new drugs that are being prescribed to the patient.

Life sciences marketers target hospitals, ambulatory surgical centers, clinics, rehabilitation centers, urgent care facilities and many more medical offices that are designated as a healthcare operation (HCO). When life sciences companies seek to reach medical professionals at HCOs, the POC exchanges that are conducted with the HCPs within the organization enrich their patient care experience.

The digital journey of a provider within an EHR system

When identifying HCPs at the POC, marketers are crafting campaigns that deploy messages to reach them effectively during their workflow. Digital strategies enable marketers to move beyond physicians' offices and care facilities to execute more meaningful interactions that will resonate with an HCP. From virtual waiting rooms to diagnosis to prescribing a therapy, the online journey for providers is a complex route for marketers to navigate and construct a messaging campaign around.

For organizations, the connection with clinicians is instrumental in the number of prescriptions being written for patients. To garner traction about a brand's drug, the messages must be crafted and shared when the content is most valuable — at the POC. This approach delves heavily on providing HCPs with educational content within the digital mediums as they care for their patient. As a prescriber interacts with their patients, marketers are tasked with creating a program that identifies the moments during the physician's workflow that are most impactful to deploy a message too. Further, when marketers operate with POC networks, the messages and timing must correlate to the platform on which the designated content is being distributed to the HCP. It reflects how when dealing with HCP campaigns, all facets of the messaging efforts must be aligned to garner optimal outcomes for the brand.

> Consequently, a patient-centric marketing model for pharmaceutical brands forgoes communications with HCPs and directly facilitates messages to patients to cultivate their education pertaining to their health. In these instances, marketing efforts are derived to engage the target audience to raise awareness about the brand's drug, medical device, research studies or therapies. This empowers the person to conduct their own research, just as consumers being targeted by online retailers during their e-commerce experience. Therefore, the patient is being served with content during their virtual visit that reflects their health circumstances being addressed with their physician.

When communications are conveyed directly to patients, then they are more prepared for discussions with their doctor. So, when a message about a particular drug or therapy is displayed within a telehealth portal while they are meeting with their doctor, the patient enquires about those options as it relates to their health. The advancement of a patient's knowledge during POC messaging initiatives spurs more in-depth conversations with their provider about all their medical treatment and prescription possibilities that can improve their health.

Patients who have researched their condition prior to the consultation come prepared for discussions with their physician. So, marketing not only expands the mindfulness of those consumers but also introduces new learnings. The ability to enrich the intelligence of patients ensures they are asking proper questions concerning their circumstances, thus enhancing the line of communication between physicians and their patients. With informative materials being shared on the patient's side of the screen, companies serve as an added resource to support the exchanges that take place throughout an online visit.

Whether it's about targeting HCPs or patients, cultivating a data-driven campaign is the basis for a strong foundation that garners positive outcomes for a company planning a POC program. Regardless of the audience, data analytics is instrumental in physician point-of-care messaging efforts. With insights on behaviors and communication preferences, moments of greatest impact are collected and then the informative materials being shared within the digital ecosystem further transform the online care that's taking place. The metrics obtained via interactions within digital point-of-care platforms illustrate a comprehensive landscape of the synergy that is cultivated between brands and their target audience. Across the various online mediums that are utilized for virtual care, the data amassed provides a thorough understanding of the personalization capabilities that can be leveraged for an effective campaign.

Digital communications at the POC formulate more meaningful exchanges between physicians and their patients, fostering a trusting relationship that leads individuals towards better health. As point-of-care messaging programs are articulated across online networks, the messages and physician's workflow equip marketers with the familiarity to strategically plan and execute their next campaign.

> Messages at the POC reach HCPs during decision-making moments to garner the greatest impact.

The collaborative roles of life sciences brands and health information technology (HIT) platforms set the stage for point-of-care messaging campaigns. Businesses in the space spanning pharmaceutical and healthcare organizations turn to digital POC messaging programs to raise awareness of their messages in a precise manner. When companies develop communication plans, point-of-care networks provide an optimal avenue to deliver content to HCPs to drive their company's business objectives for the campaign. Whether it's to boost script lift or increase awareness about the latest therapies, the POC is where corporations institute procedures to affirm personalization practices to connect with providers.

At the heart of POC platforms is the opportunity to reach HCPs in real time while they are tending to patients. Thus, the added support throughout the physician-patient conversation is aided by brands that utilize the communication channels appropriately. The content deployed during virtual care moments positions organizations to be relevant during the workflow of the provider when the messages conveyed resonate with them during their interaction with their patients. With online communications, HCPs can interact with brands on their own terms.

A reported **92% of physicians noted the inefficiency of EHR systems** that included pop-ups and excessive scrolling that attributed a negative impact on their ability to deliver high-quality care.[8] For companies in the category, POC networks open the ability to be step-for-step with physicians with exchanges that don't disrupt their dialogue with their patients but equip them with educational assets to share with individuals leading up to and after their diagnosis.

The messaging formats being offered by the platforms have an integral role in POC messaging campaigns. Whether it's a telehealth, eRx, EHR or an EHR app, the HIT platform must formularize the messaging formats in which the content can appear within the online mediums. The structure of the platforms lays out the ways companies can communicate with physicians. Thus, it's imperative that the offerings of a platform showcase messages in a fashion and at moments when the value is highest for organizations. When businesses align with a partner to distribute their marketing campaigns, then the comprehension of how their channel runs messages is critical to set the foundation for selecting systems that will be utilized for serving messages as part of the campaign.

I'll delve deeper into each platform later in the book, as the basis for the marketing campaign being deployed in a designated medium is determined to achieve optimal results, that is, how the message is displayed and when it is critical to the success of communications to an HCP. HIT platforms are relied on to facilitate messages in a way that leads to better business outcomes. When the road to the physician is disrupted with content that directs them to another screen and in the process their attention moves from their patients, the ecosystem fails to reach the benefits that are achievable in the space. However, when the path of the provider flows with relevant messages that align with the health circumstances of their patients, well then that's POC messaging at its finest.

02

THE EVOLUTION OF POINT-OF-CARE MESSAGING

Point-of-care messaging has come a long way from how it used to happen earlier in the traditional manner to how it is done now with the advent of digital technologies.

From sharing posters, stickers and calendars about the latest drugs and therapeutic research, point-of-care messaging has transformed over time. Those marketing materials in physical form were then commonly shared by life sciences companies with physicians to raise awareness about the most recent developments in the market and create a top-of-the-mind recall for the prescriber while treating a patient. They were either branded or unbranded messages intending to impart knowledge towards patient care.

The progression of digital solutions for the life sciences space received a significant emphasis with initiatives set forth to incentivize hospitals and providers to adopt EHR systems in 2009 as part of the Health Information Technology for Economic and Clinical Health (HITECH) Act.[9] To drive the transition to online platforms, HITECH allocated $35 billion[10] to encourage hospitals and HCPs to promote and expand digital EHR systems and related technologies. The move was aimed at reforming the healthcare category with online solutions.

When the Affordable Care Act (ACA) was passed in 2010, it marked a crucial early stage for digital POC networks. It commenced the marketing phenomenon that progressed brand messages to move through virtual mediums too. The ACA was created to improve the quality of healthcare and health insurance to American citizens. In addition, it set the course to regulate the health insurance industry and reduce healthcare-related spending in the United States.

With **70% of medical decisions based on laboratory results**,[11] obligations from ACA established the foundation for the use of EHR systems to share lab test results. With the progression to utilize EHR networks, an avenue of communications got created for clinicians while they viewed the laboratory results in order to prescribe a therapy to their patients.

The Affordable Care Act ushered in the digital marketing era within EHR systems.

With EHR systems being at the forefront of the new-age online solutions, the information about a patient's visit equipped marketers with the opportunity to better understand a physician's practice. It's important to comprehend how exactly that happens. The understanding of the clinical history of a clinician's EHR workflow aids marketers to serve them personalized messages within their EHR workflow, enriching the dialogue held with their patients.

The superior healthcare model backs marketers with data-driven insights from EHR platforms that have altered the way life sciences brands comprehend a patient's visit to their caregivers. These learnings are used to identify how interactions impact the workflow of their target audience. From tracking wait times, patient requests and the length of appointments, the data obtained from within the EHR networks nurtures the promise for virtual care exchanges. It is seen that the optimal moment to communicate with providers is during the patient visits, and the capacity of EHR mediums to facilitate messages progresses the value EHR channels bring to the digital point-of-care ecosystem. With the polices of the ACA in place, **96% of hospitals and 84% of practices document** their patient records electronically.[12]

Digital marketing: growing with new opportunities to reach HCP

The digital path, however, was not elevated in an instant with the influx of resources from the HITECH Act as electronic prescriptions represented only **25% of the prescriptions being dispensed in 2013**.[13] Life sciences brands had to navigate the value proposition messages at the POC would deliver. Marketers had to identify the type of content physicians were open to receiving to foster relationships via the exchanges that were tailored to the prescriber. All of that to embolden the ability of prescribers to provide high-quality care without disrupting the patient's visit.

The digital landscape evolved the way marketers communicate with clinicians via online systems. With the new clinical pathways at the POC put in place by the ACA and the Physician Payment Sunshine Act (PPSA), the progression for digital point-of-care began when the regulations came into effect in 2013. As data collection commenced, the policy was implemented for greater transparency around financial relationships between physicians and life sciences companies to ensure providers didn't have a conflict of interest that was reflective of their prescribing behaviors.

As part of the ACA, the PPSA signified the first Congressional involvement around regulations for pharmaceutical marketing. This was sought to protect against any bias in an HCP's decision-making that would undercut the clinical research being conducted within the industry. The regulations elevated transparency as it required disclosing partnerships between organizations and HCPs to benefit the industry.

Prior to the ACA, messaging initiatives to reach providers at the POC sparked inventive tactics to facilitate communications within doctors' offices. Entered then Triple i, a part of MediMedia and MediScripts, which brought a fresh opportunity for life sciences brands to connect with clinicians via prescription pads. While marketers were exploring measures to reach their target audience digitally, the introduction of content displayed within prescription pads garnered unprecedented access to medical professionals at a 100% open rate.

 The ability to reach HCPs at decision-making moments with marketing materials is powerful resource for brands.

As the new means for communications during that period, branded and unbranded messages appeared on the cover of the prescription pad and throughout on every fifth prescription page. With this forward-thinking solution, MediScripts introduced the latest messaging opportunity at the POC that would go on to boost the NRx per doctor and new prescribers. The company's resourceful idea increased script lift, and measured sizable impact gained while effectively facilitating messages at the point-of-care.

The creative mode of communication instilled the power to reach HCPs during decision-making moments that was tailored to their specialty. This presented the opportunity in the market for brands to seamlessly interact with providers in a manner that was fluid with their workflow and paved the way for future messaging strategies that would launch cutting-edge campaigns.

Prescription pads were a necessity for physicians to operate at the time. However, providers had to budget to cover the expense of the prescription pads. Companies brought to the market a way to provide clinicians with prescription pads at no cost. And, when the prescriber ran out of pads, another set would be delivered with new content directed towards the provider's specialty. This practice was altered though when the PPSA was passed. This policy prevented companies from providing free prescription pads to HCPs.

The intuitive method of communication had imparted brands with the power to reach HCPs at moments when the therapy is being discussed. It opened opportunities to seamlessly access providers with communications that didn't disrupt their workflow. This approach would come to play a pivotal role of defining marketing strategies for future digital point-of-care marketing campaigns.

While MediaScripts served as an early example of the value of messages being distributed within prescription pads, DrFirst and RXNT would take the digital approach for facilitating prescriptions electronically and became early adopters for deploying messaging solutions on POC platforms. By 2013, Surescripts, the largest health information network in the United States **represented 58% of the eRx market,** which exceeded **more than one billion electronic prescriptions.**[14] That's also when Surescripts launched the first *"National Progress Report,"* which continues to analyze the category to provide an overview on the eRx landscape. Most recently, the 2020 report noted that **1.91 billion e-prescriptions were filled**, and **more than one million physicians wrote treatments electronically** for the first time in December that year.[15]

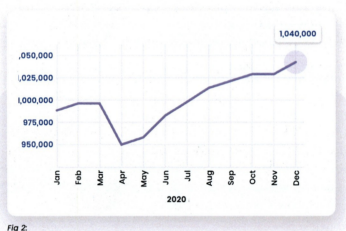

Fig 2:
Active e-prescribers by month

The transition from posters to digital wallboards in doctors' offices encapsulated the digital makeover in the industry. Physician's Weekly, which has a track record for its HCP wallboards in exam rooms at the POC, progressed to embrace digital messaging opportunities to reach physicians during the evolution of virtual care.

The use of digital screens gained traction with the use of digital visuals to support communications to physicians while they tended to their patients, whether it was health-related educational content such as illustrations detailing therapies or video of a key opinion leader sharing insights in their field or takeaways from drug research studies.

The downfalls of an emerging category

The evolution of point-of-care communications wasn't without mistakes in the competitive market, which took place with Outcome Health, a digital provider of medical information and advertising in doctors' offices. From 2012 to 2017, the company defrauded its clients by selling advertising inventory that it didn't possess.[16] During this period, Outcome Health inflated patient engagement metrics for how frequently patients engaged with the company's devices. In the end of the investigation, Outcome Health **reached an agreement with the Department of Justice** to pay $70 million to the victims of the company's fraud scheme.[17]

In 2021, Outcome Health was acquired by PatientPoint and was rebranded as PatientPoint Health Technologies. The two organizations that coordinate and manage the display of content on screens at the point-of-care within physicians' offices aligned their solutions to now support communications to nearly 150,000 HCPs, which accounts for approximately 750 million patient visits each year with those HCPs. But there was a lesson learned - the need for transparency in point-of-care communications and it was one of the valuable takeaways that has stuck with marketers.

Surescripts too came under scrutiny from the Federal Trade Commission and was sued for the **company's anti-competitive vertical and horizontal restraints in the eRx category of routing and eligibility.**[18]

Epic and Practice Fusion had a prominent reach of providers within their EHR networks that would impact the future landscape of communications within the digital space. With the upward trajectory of the industry, and massive reach for the category, these two industry players guided interactions within the point-of-care ecosystem that would have a lasting impact. Though, I'll go more in-depth about each organization in the next chapter as communications during virtual care would progress with greater intel for the direction of the usages of the platforms.

As the value of data within POC mediums increased, the Open, Public, Electronic, and Necessary Government Data (OPEN) Act was passed to boost efforts for data transparency and support organizations to properly track, manage and publish their data sets. When it came into law in 2019, it marked the first time that non-sensitive government data should be in the open from the onset, while still ensuring data privacy protection of individuals. In addition, it required data to be accessible in machine-readable formats, which enabled the transition from paper documents and out-of-date filing systems towards digital solutions to streamline data sharing.

When EHR metrics are cultivated, greater insights are gathered about HCPs, their usage of telehealth platforms, communication practices, prescribing behaviors and much more to set the foundation to target audiences. As the analysis of physician-patient interactions takes place, the communications approach is being refined to deliver messages to providers in a manner that's reflective of their preferences.

The OPEN Act unlocked EHR data on larger EHR applications, driving utilization of available data sets to improve patient care and usher in new abilities for marketing initiatives at the point-of-care. With the gathering of digital records, point-of-care marketing would begin to gain prominence with telehealth platforms being utilized for virtual consultations.

As new policies and regulations are introduced, marketers and organizations must adjust to the guidelines. Prior to the ACA being passed, only **12% of hospitals had adopted EHRs**, which now is at **96% of hospitals** across the United States.[19] As physicians switch their pen and pad for digital tools, the potential for POC messaging will be realized. With advancements of data transparency within the space, the communication tactics are getting enriched to reach HCPs more effectively.

Digital, fueling better health outcomes

With the adoption of virtual platforms to conduct patient visits, digital solutions have become essential for life sciences brands to reach HCPs. The non-personal distribution of physical materials by organizations to enable physicians to learn and be reminded about treatment options has made way for digital content to be accessible in real-time for providers to advise patients. Messages pertaining to an individual's health were never a one-size-fits-all approach to instruct a person on their path to better health results. The nature of content that's succinctly delivered to HCPs simply lacked personalization that would become formidable in today's virtual environment.

Breaking through to physicians at the point-of-care is not an easy feat. Organizations have been challenged with ways to connect with clinicians when they are most receptive to information. With the status quo of marketing materials being distributed to HCPs, companies weren't maximizing the ability to cultivate a meaningful connection with physicians to build trust in their drugs that would benefit their patients and drive script lift. Physicians were overwhelmed with printed assets being shared to gain awareness. Now they had online messages that were more accommodating and beneficial to better educate themselves and their patients.

The greater amount of activity within the point-of-care ecosystem empowered marketers in the space to gain a stronger perspective on the impact messages within POC channels could have. With active online campaigns taking place, the data points were being collected to better target the right prescribers and identify the right moment to send a message. At this junction, telehealth interactions became a viable resource to refine the way exchanges happened with physicians to have it reflect their discussions with patients for driving better health outcomes.

The conversion from print to digital was a slow process for the life sciences category, but then the Covid-19 pandemic accelerated a transition in digital point-of-care marketing for brands. Without the availability of company representatives to meet with HCPs in-person, the adoption of virtual messages rapidly spread out of necessity to communicate with providers. In April 2020, the use of telehealth platforms for office visits and outpatient care jumped **up to 78 times higher than February of that year**.[20] Further, **84% of providers were using eRx platforms** in 2020.[21]

> Prior to the Covid-19 pandemic, telehealth was readily available for consumers with **74% of employers offering telemedicine coverage in 2018**.[22] However, only **2.4% of employees used the service** at that time.[23]

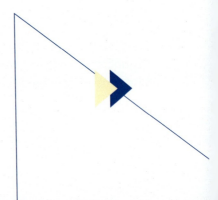

As an industry that was slow to embrace digital messaging technologies, the Covid-19 pandemic fast-tracked the adoption of online marketing solutions by years.

As the pandemic increased the use of point-of-care platforms for virtual care, marketers in the life sciences category had to adjust to and even embrace digital messaging that had already been widely adopted across other industries for marketing campaigns. With reports that up to **$250 billion in healthcare spending** could be digitized,[24] marketers had to refine their online messaging tactics to optimize interactions with HCPs within digital channels.

The embrace of virtual care during the Covid-19 outbreak streamlined communication operations to reflect the burgeoning market. As data sets are being compiled, marketers will be able to better comprehend the pain points, behaviors and preferences of clinicians throughout the POC ecosystem. During the pandemic, the virtual care channels were adopted by providers to reach their patients during the tumultuous period. The familiarity with the platforms didn't just expand for providers and patients, but for marketers as well. The messaging habits developed during the unprecedented time will formulate the future aspects of point-of-care messaging to providers that will drive business outcomes in the latest paradigm.

As of April 2021, **58% of physicians viewed virtual care more favorably than prior to the pandemic and 84% of doctors offered a telehealth visit.**[25] The revolution of digital messaging is only scratching the surface and data analytics has huge capabilities to emrich HCP communications. The data-based decisions of marketers will formulate new methods to reach providers with greater efficiency and effectiveness to embolden organizations to achieve their business objectives.

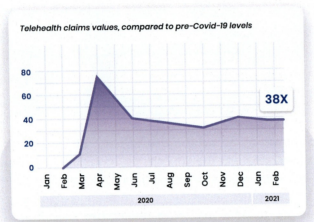

Fig 3: *Growth in telehealth usage peaked during April 2020 but has since stabilized*

Innovative solutions will vitalize exchanges in the point-of-care environment to make greater headway to reach prescribers during decisive moments of care. The physician-patient relationship stands to benefit from the restructuring of digital communication campaigns across the point-of-care platforms to influence positively the interactions brands have with HCPs.

03

TYPES OF POINT-OF-CARE MESSAGING

Point-of-care messages need to be delivered with relevance and precision to provoke the interest of clinicians during patient interactions. For life sciences marketers, the type of communication that takes place with an HCP should reflect the current phase of their digital journey within the point-of-care ecosystem. The content being shared with providers is essential to elevate their knowledge throughout their workflow to better educate and advise their patients.

To lay the foundation for a campaign that will optimize results, it's a necessity for companies to craft messages that are insightful for prescribers to improve patient care.

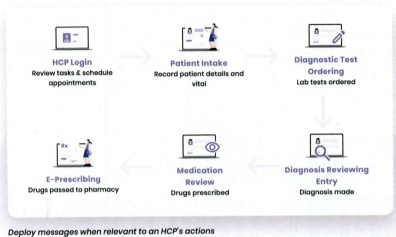

Deploy messages when relevant to an HCP's actions

Therefore, it's essential to take into consideration various types of messages to distinguish the opportunities for when clinical messaging, clinical triggers, patient affordability messaging and workflow messaging are beneficial to integrate with communication efforts to achieve an organization's desired business objectives.

When hypertargeting messages to HCPs, marketers are equipped with the ability to customize interactions that are relevant to the physician's journey. By understanding the significance of the types of messages, life sciences brands can align messages within campaigns to be distributed via appropriate online platforms to effectively reach their target audience.

Understand the value each type of POC messaging offers to strategically deploy messaging campaigns.

Also, marketers must factor in the type of messages to distribute, and that if they are branded or unbranded. Communication efforts can be built around the benefits of a drug or treatment. Another consideration is to take an unbranded approach for a campaign or align on a balance between branded and unbranded messages to support the company's intentions during a messaging program.

For unbranded efforts, organizations gain the advantage of being able to raise awareness about developments pertaining to a disease, treatment, industry research and additional subject matters that may impact the therapy an HCP advises to the patient.

By considering these elements when devising the recency and frequency of content to serve to providers, campaigns can be deployed within POC networks to connect with HCPs at critical points during their digital journey.

Clinical Messaging

As communications take place throughout POC channels, clinical messaging needs to be a cohesive endeavor among life sciences marketers to align messages to reflect the information being discussed between a prescriber and the patient. The real-time exchanges are essential to support the HCP's prescribing decisions while discussing a treatment plan.

> Look at how Amazon's Alexa gathers a consumer's information throughout the day to identify their interests so a personalized message can be served to them. That message is a targeted one, helping the consumer decide about proceeding with the purchase. This is what clinical messaging does – it considers the behavior and actions of an HCP and then displays them a message based on those attributes.

Whether it's their latest chart, an update to a patient's status or a diagnosis, communications can be conveyed throughout the patient's virtual care experience while HCPs review clinical messages in EHR platforms. Therefore, the messages being distributed to the clinician during their digital interactions need to be informative to guide the prescriber towards actions that will benefit the individual. The provider's mindset when receiving clinical messages is focused on treating their patient. So, the contextual relevance of the exchanges is essential to garner the attention of clinicians at the point-of-care.

An example of clinical messaging

Consequently, the content needs to follow suit with exchanges that will heighten the awareness about drugs and therapies that are relevant for the individual's condition. By having educational materials shared with an HCP during these decision-making moments, it empowers them with the capacity to enrich their expertise in real-time about their patient's conditions and also to take the person through their therapy options. The supportive resources for the physician who already has access to the patient's medical records at their fingertips will then lead to more well-rounded determinations, so any oversights when instructing the patient on a treatment plan can be avoided.

Clinical Triggers

When a provider accesses a patient's chart, the dialogue needs to be tailored to the individual's circumstances. Thus, having messages triggered basis pre-determined criteria of the patient's health background, diagnosis or therapy are fundamental to uplift the medical discussions being held. So that when lab orders are placed, or procedure codes are fed in the system, then optimal communications for treatment can be displayed. With a rule-based measure in place, messages are deployed going by the actions of the HCP to support his need. This practice positions brands to deliver specific medical information to physicians that correlates with their practicing specialty.

> During a telehealth visit, clinical triggers are an effective tool to empower marketers with the ability to serve messages within digital platforms during a patient's interaction with their clinician. Once HCPs access the login screen to kick off their digital journey with an individual, clinical triggers can begin to deploy educational messages during the patient consultation portion of the visit up until the eRx stage.

The usage of clinical triggers enables life sciences businesses to supply the latest drug research and therapies to physicians to share them with their patients.

Being part of the provider's workflow emboldens marketers to remain connected with their target audience during decisive occasions for the individual's health.

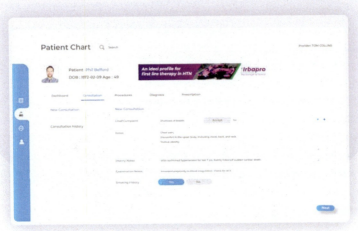

An example of a clinical trigger ad

Also, organizations must balance the way clinical triggers are served in order to not disrupt the physician's attention from their patients. At its finest, these messages reach HCPs at decision-making moments, whether it's when the diagnosis is first determined or upon seeking a therapy to prescribe to the individual. The connection with a piece of content has the capacity to resonate with the HCP to provide optimal treatment to their patients.

Patient Affordability Messaging

Approximately 18 million U.S. adults were reported to be unable to pay for at least one doctor-prescribed medication for their household during the three months prior to a study that was conducted in 2021.[26] The access to patient assistance programs and co-pay cards for prescriptions is a crucial message that when shared with HCPs can be communicated to their patient. The awareness that is raised about patient assistance offerings available to individuals is one that can act as the differentiator if medication adherence is achieved or not with a patient. Afterall, 33% of patients have intentionally skipped filling a prescription because of its high price.[27]

When physicians reach the eRx stage of a visit, then advising their patient on their financial options is a pivotal moment of the virtual care experience. While it may be perceived as going beyond their medical responsibilities, the comprehension of the monetary position of an individual may be a determining factor in the outcome of their health.

With knowledge about the financial implications that surround the drug being prescribed, the consideration for alternative medicines that offer the same health results will evolve the prescriber's views on the treatments with the awareness on patient assistance offerings to consider for their patient.

A person's monetary circumstance may not be at the forefront of the provider's mind. However, that is an area that the medical professional is able to decipher during their consultation. However, as the two individuals discuss a treatment plan, messages that are brought to the attention of an HCP within a digital channel will assist in having a better rapport to generate dialogue along the financial terms of the prescription. Therefore, the messages that reach HCPs drive medication adherence and facilitate the communications between the provider and their patient, so a therapy can be reached that is achievable for the individual.

An example of a patient affordability message

The socio-economic status of a patient can become a barrier for their visit to a physician with the out-of-pocket expense one endures without health insurance. To overcome the hardship, the uninsured person stands to benefit from learning about patient assistance programs via their provider while conversing about the prescribed drugs that are a part of their therapy. By passing on patient assistance to a person, HCPs are driving a positive influence on their patients to prevent prescription abandonment.

 Educating HCPs about financial assistance programs available for prescriptions can drive medication adherence with their patients.

Workflow Messaging

The advanced era of digital point-of-care messaging campaigns delivers content that's relevant to the prescriber during their online workflow. The facilitation of non-disruptive communications can optimize the physician's experience with an online EHR medium.

Whether it's during login, diagnosis, reviewing lab results or eRx within an EHR system, continual exchanges during an HCP's workflow are advantageous to the medical care that can be delivered to their patients. By being virtually alongside prescribers, the interactions reflect the phase of the visit, and the resources that will be of the highest value to the provider. Further, the real-time measurement of communications empowers marketers to analyze the moments during the clinician's journey when the messages are most effective.

While HCPs are active on their EHR platform, point-of-care messaging initiatives can cultivate a deeper familiarity around ailments, diseases, drugs, treatments and much more within their specialty to apply to their patient interaction. When cultivating messages at the point-of-care, the timing and relevance of the communications in the physician's workflow dictate the type of exchanges that have a greater likelihood of achieving the sought-after business objectives.

Thus, setting a cadence to control the moments for when designated messages are shared with HCPs elevates the relevancy for when a prescriber comes across the communications. Being aligned with the mentality of a prescriber as they proceed to converse with their patients enables the messages to resonate based on the juncture of the virtual visit.

An example of an ad during an HCP's workflow

Reaching prescribers when they are inclined to act on the message elevates the care afforded to individuals that will improve their health outcomes. Also, the conversations are then more engaging with their physician about their medical circumstance. Which is why the use of data analytics boosts the traction of digital exchanges by pinpointing the moments during an HCP's workflow when the person is most receptive to messages from brands. A provider's preferences and behaviors during their workflow are valuable insights that Artificial Intelligence (AI) can capture. They can be deciphered into actionable insights.

When marketers are equipped with metrics, the deployment of messages are strategically laid out throughout the HCP's workflow. The digital ecosystem is complex, so grasping a firm understanding of the messages at designated points of HCP's journey signifies which exchanges are most beneficial to be facilitated to optimize communication efforts.

With the distinction on the kinds of content to drive business outcomes during the workflow, marketers can implement a data-driven approach that reflects the metrics of previous campaigns for more efficient communications across the optimal virtual network. When life sciences brands embrace data analytics for POC messaging campaigns, the communication landscape to reach HCPs becomes clearer.

Delivering Point-of-Care Messaging

In the instance of an organization sharing details about a co-pay card with the physician at the patient consultation period for a drug may swiftly become irrelevant if the drug isn't the prescription written by the clinician. Further, the details about patient assistance aren't top-of-mind early on during the visit as the provider wants to understand the patient's medical history as they proceed with an examination to assess their current symptoms. Thus, the traction of a message is elevated when the treatment decision is being made and the eRx is processed to a pharmacy. Patient assistance options can be presented to the patient via their physician to determine the therapy that the patient is most likely to adhere to. During these moments, a financial-themed message being displayed to the HCP encourages those conversations with their patients to cover all the aspects of the treatment and ensures monetary support is available when necessary for an individual. The timeliness of a useful exchange is a contributing factor in the type of health outcomes that will be garnered for individuals.

As informative assets appear throughout the digital workflow of physicians, the lines of communications among life sciences brands, providers and patients have a promising stream of information flow that enriches the virtual care experience. When knowledge is expanded throughout the category in a seamless manner that aligns with the treatment missions for a clinician, then the collaboration benefits all parties involved.

04

THE HCP-PATIENT RELATIONSHIP
AT THE POINT-OF-CARE

The transformation of point-of-care messaging for online mediums has deepened the HCP-patient relationship. Trust is primary for a meaningful HCP-patient connection. So, to strengthen the bond between the two individuals, an open line of fluid communication needs to be established. During virtual visits, the conversations that progress from diagnosis to the advised therapy must be well intentioned for better health results.

To do so, physicians must be well-versed in the prescribed treatment, along with alternative options to instruct a person accordingly on their path to recovery and tailor the interaction during the consultation to reflect their medical circumstance.

> Therefore, life sciences brands have an integral role to help providers with a vast array of educational content that concerns their patients to support their medical discussions. By nurturing an HCP's knowledge with an ongoing flow of helpful messages pertaining to their specialty, the influx of specifics about the latest developments in the field enriches the conversations held during consultations.

Patients arrive to their visit with the belief that their HCP is knowledgeable about all potential conditions in their medical field, along with an immense familiarity of the drugs, and potential side effects of the medicines. However, as new drugs enter the market and research progresses with medical treatments that are available in the space, physicians may not be aware of the most recent information that's pertinent for their patients. So, point-of-care channels offer the opportunity to reach HCPs as they are interacting with their patients to share tailored information that resonates with them as they are communicating with their patients.

> Traditionally, the physician-patient interaction used to dominate because of the ample trust that used to get built on meeting each other in-person and talking about things beyond health issues.
> Then devices came in. It cut the time spent on interactions as HCPs began spending time with the devices too during a consultation. This led to disturbance in the patient-physician relationship. With POC messaging, I believe brands have an opportunity to trigger quality conversations between physicians and their patients that could help build the relationship and hence the trust.

Clinicians need to effectively connect with patients, which can pose a challenge during virtual care visits. For HCPs to connect to an individual, life sciences organizations can facilitate interactions that are customized to their target audience. For point-of-care campaigns, it's important for life sciences brands to realize the value of personalized content being shared to enhance the quality discussions physicians can have with their patients.

When marketers leverage messaging formats within POC platforms, then a person's mindset is at ease knowing the conversations they are having with their prescriber are being supported with the latest healthcare information in their field. For an effective communication plan, the benefits need to be passed through the physician to have the health improvements come to fruition during the patient's experience. As a person goes through a consultation with their provider, an understanding of their ailments need to be grasped by the prescriber to arrive at a therapy that's most suitable to address the health circumstance of the individual.

> Individualized communications to HCPs are significant resources that build the foundation for the HCP-patient relationships. Messaging being served as prescribers navigate point-of-care channels aids providers and unifies the faith patients have during their treatment process. While patients join a telehealth portal seeking the professional expertise of a physician, their provider may not have all the answers. So, it's important for the shared content to be part of the prescriber's workflow that expands their expertise with the latest drugs, therapies, research studies, side effects, and any additional inquires that are asked by a patient. When communications are distributed within digital channels, virtual care is elevated, and connections are fostered as clinicians can remain engaged with the individual. Having access to additional medical resources is paramount to achieve the confidence in the patient that the provider's direction will lead them towards better health results.

A key to execute the delivery of messages within POC networks is for marketers to not disrupt the physician's workflow within the platform. When communications come across the point-of-care channel, then language such as "click here to learn more" should not be associated with any campaign. An HCP's attention should never be taken away from their patient while viewing digital messages and transferred out of their telehealth or EHR system to another digital channel. A brief communication that delivers insights to the physician should be displayed in the current screen the provider is on and guide them towards an online outlet to obtain additional information once the patient visit has concluded.

The marketer's conviction should be to pursue campaign tactics to effectively reach their target audience, and not to secure a click-through to another online medium. The high value return for marketers is the confidence that will be gained with patients as their HCP efficiently advises them on their health circumstance.

While I was tending to a patient, I wanted to give the person my undivided attention. The notion that an HCP is preoccupied with another task during a virtual visit can deter the person's confidence in their prescriber. So, communications across virtual mediums need to be devised carefully to ensure the physician has full attention towards their patients. The facilitation of messages needs to be non-disruptive to the journey of the prescriber.

The messages being dispensed within the virtual channels should be distributed in a manner that it doesn't interfere with a clinician's interaction with a patient. So, the messages must appear on the screen that's seamlessly integrated within the channel and not have the content overwhelm or distract the prescriber from tending to their patient to jeopardize that connection.

The educational assets will embolden the relationship between the two parties with the latest information in the field, strengthening the trust the clinician gains with their patient. With the bond fortified, clinicians have a greater possibility to improve a patient's behavior to adhere to the prescribed therapy and provide a high-value virtual care experience in the process.

George C.D. Griffith
EVP, Omnichannel Strategy at Relevate Health
Co-Founder of ConneXion360

The imaginative Greeks created myths to explain just about every element of the human condition. Fast forward to present, and as a culture, myths are ever present.

There isn't a week that passes by that I don't find myself in a conversation with a Brand Leader or an MLR (Medical Legal Regulatory) point person asking a question around a misperception &/or myth associated with EHR/Point-of-Care Marketing.

Point-of-Care HCP engagement should be considered as an HCP activation solution for most of all brands. Within the EHR, we as marketers can educate and remind our target customers about the key attributes of our product/device while they are seeing the right patient at the point-of-care.

This chapter should be printed &/or kept digitally on your desktop so that when one of these myths come up, you now have a definitive resource to dispel these misperceptions accordingly.

05

THE ADVANCEMENT OF MEASUREMENT TECHNOLOGIES FOR IMPACTFUL MESSAGING

The impact of a point-of-care messaging initiatives must be quantified to recognize the effectiveness of the messages reaching HCPs. Without advanced measurement tools in place, marketers spend their marketing budget disproportionately through the digital ecosystem. In the unpredictable point-of-care environment, the use of data analytics to support well-rounded strategies put in place by life sciences brands is essential for successful communication programs.

As ad spending in the U.S. increased year-over-year in 2021 by 21.6% up to $36.3 billion,[28] the data-related spending, which includes measurement, identity, analytics and attribution, also increased year-over-year in 2021 up to 26% to $29.3 billion.[29] Measurement tools provide comprehensive indication of the content's performance to formulate an approach for communications that maximize the effectiveness and efficiency of messaging initiatives. By identifying high-performing elements of communication efforts, organizations can allocate their budgets and resources to establish the framework to examine the progress and input data-based tactics to achieve the desired business objectives.

Life sciences category is in a period with abundant data and technologies that equip organizations with data-based insights from messaging campaigns. However, measurement solutions for the sector have progressed to showcase the ROI that's achievable and correlate the results directly to virtual interactions that were executed. Also, it's vital to note the ability to obtain transparent metrics that can inform the organization when a campaign is missing the mark.

Embrace the learnings that are obtainable via campaign metrics to construct data-driven messaging tactics.

Now, I'll take a closer look at the state of measurement technologies for marketers in the life sciences industry.

Measurement solutions aid point-of-care communications

To reach HCPs, the life sciences marketing approach evolved from a mass market design to adopting the implementation of measurement tools that empowered companies to aim for a niche audience.

While marketers had previously taken a mass marketing approach to reach HCPs, the progression of measurement solutions enables organizations to better identify the clinicians they want to reach. With data analytics, marketers are emboldened to extend their messages that HCPs relate with. For performance marketing programs to garner an impact in the market, businesses can position messages to a specific segment of providers instead of a broader audience to achieve the maximum benefit.

> Data analytics help organizations to better decipher the results of messaging campaigns. With knowledge on the parameters of the message and the forum in which it was received, marketers can measure the business outcomes that were attained and narrow down the successes of exchanges to HCPs to particular elements of a campaign.

With precision capabilities being paramount for marketers, the refined data-based strategies set forth the ability to improve the approach of communications that would generate a higher ROI.

Embracing measurement tools for personalized messages

With the need to deliver messages pertaining to a clinician's medical field, acquiring data sets to tailor messages was a necessity to continue the progression of point-of-care communications. The ability to understand the interests, behaviors, preferences and needs of a person was a significant step to achieve the type of point-of-care communications that clinicians experience today.

By advancing measurement efforts to collect and examine the communication metrics of campaigns, the data points obtained can lead marketers to optimize the results of interactions. Just like in the consumer market, when it comes to exchanges at the POC, the messages need to resonate with an individual and have those shared during the appropriate moment of a person's digital journey.

The acquisition of physician-level data led the measurement of messaging efforts to pinpoint prescribers who should be targeted with messages. Consequently, marketers have the ability to narrow down audiences to identify the relevant HCPs for the distributed messages. Also, measurement solutions need to distinguish the point-of-care platforms that are garnering the most impactful interactions with clinicians. While clinicians navigate digital channels, data analytics are utilized to further enhance personalization of communications by deciphering the stages during a physician's journey when the deployed exchanges are achieving the highest recognition with an individual.

Therefore, the ability to track the needs and preferences of an HCP elevates the quality of communications that are introduced into their digital workflow. The insights garnered from the interactions lead marketers to produce a more comprehensive and tailored approach to how campaigns will be executed to effectively reach clinicians on a personalized level.

Establishing long-lasting relationships with HCPs via informative messages

Marketers must recognize the messages that hit the mark with HCPs as their workflow takes them across the digital point-of-care spectrum. Being able to measure the impact of communications with their target audience empowers the messaging strategies to achieve the desired outcomes.

Therefore, measurement technologies need to be utilized to afford companies with the aptitude to comprehend which content is being taken in by their target audience and recognize the manner they are absorbing the messages. To examine the reception of the communications is crucial to formulate programs that will build long-lasting relationships with HCPs.

A clinician's time is valuable, but in their profession it's a necessity to continue their education and remain up-to date with the latest developments within their medical field. With informative materials being served to HCPs, companies stand to establish their role as an education provider for clinicians to help them with the latest research and drugs around their specialty. As data-based insights complement prescribers during their workflow, more meaningful and long-lasting relationships will develop.

> Strengthen relationships with HCPs by sharing timely and relevant educational materials that pertain to the clinician's specialty.

Advancing messaging intelligence with AI

The current use rate of AI is projected to rise from 4% to 18% in marketing and sales efforts during the next few years.[30] The data capturing an HCP's behaviors and prescribing habits was once physical documents within medical facilities, but now the digital pathway has afforded the opportunity to collect data analytics to progress the intelligence of point-of-care campaigns. With the use of AI in POC communications, the data sets are examined to equip corporations with greater intelligence about the scope of messaging initiatives. By doing so, data-based decision-making can be incorporated into messaging strategies to advance business objectives.

With AI shaping the landscape of point-of-care interactions, brands are prepared with an all-encompassing perspective on the impact of digital exchanges that are being deployed to HCPs. As data is collected throughout the point-of-care ecosystem, insights are gathered to illustrate the pathway to connect with a company's target audience and comprehend the next steps that can be taken to articulate communications that will boost results.

Taking messaging efforts to new heights with advanced measurement solutions

Tracking the performance of campaigns is quintessential to maximize the technological resources that are available to an organization to implement communication tactics. With the benefits of AI and machine learning (ML) technologies, the proficiency of a communication program is superior with the comprehensive solution supporting the delivery of content.

The digital world has progressed with advanced solutions to enhance the measurement capabilities of point-of-care messaging efforts. Communication gaps can arise as marketers facilitate virtual campaigns across various facets of the medical field. Therefore, precise metrics that are collected delve deeper into the efficiency of the messages that are being distributed within point-of-care networks.

AI and ML solutions embolden personalization within messaging projects and 84% of digital marketers leaders stated they believe using AI/ML enhances the marketing function's ability to deliver real-time, personalized experiences to customers.[31] With the support of ML technologies, patterns can be detected within communications across point-of-care networks to boost messaging outcomes via the acquired data analytics. The recognition of trends can empower marketers to operate campaigns more proficiently by optimizing the length of programs and the usage of selected channels based on the data learnings.

The progression of real-time measurement technologies

Marketers no longer have to wait to see if their brand experienced script lift during the duration of a campaign. The use of physical marketing collateral that was present within exam and waiting rooms didn't offer the ability to measure the impact of a campaign in real time. The real-time measurement capabilities within point-of-care platforms increase the aptitude of marketers across the category with data analytics on the messages, audience reach, script lift, preferred communication channel of HCPs and additional metrics.

The anytime-anywhere mindset for virtual care opens the potential to understand the way HCPs communicate with messages during their digital journey. For point-of-care messaging campaigns, the digital ecosystem is complex, so the progress to have up-to-date insights is monumental for marketers to optimize their communications approach. Now, measurement tools can dictate online platforms that garner the highest ROI. When a measurement solution reports the figures are lower than expected, the allotted budget for that portion of the campaign can be designated to a higher performing area to secure greater returns. Therefore, monetary budgets aren't wasted with dispensing resources for an entire project that delivers underwhelming results.

Furthermore, the messaging, the platform that it's being delivered on, and the timing for when the communications are being facilitated are analyzed to examine the performance of the campaign, positioning companies to strengthen their future campaigns.

Marketers must avoid vanity metrics and focus on metrics that matter

The use of measurement solutions provides marketers with technological advancements to maximize business outcomes for brands. However, to do so marketers have to move beyond vanity metrics such as clicks and impressions when determining the data that's essential to collect and analyze to formulate stronger communication programs. Click-through-rates are valuable for consumer-centric initiatives, but when targeting HCPs, this metric needs to go by the wayside.

When prescribers are tending to patients and tracking their patients' visit in their EHR or conducting the consultation within a telehealth channel, their attention needs to remain present with the individual. A message shouldn't be displayed to a provider as they are viewing lab results, which encourages a click to learn more about a research study, taking them to another online medium and making them less engaged with their patient.

> Messaging campaigns within point-of-care channels need to keep the provider's attention on their patient and must not take them outside of the online platform.

The essence of a message needs to support providers at the point-of-care while not disrupting the screen experience of their digital journey. By being able to measure the communications, sequential messages at optimal moments can be shared during their workflow based on the learnings from the measurement technologies.

That's why when it comes to measurement in point-of-care campaigns, reach, frequency, share of voice, script lift and the use of coupons/co-pay cards are the insights that are valuable for companies to obtain, examine, understand and formulate campaigns around.

Measure the effectiveness of point-of-care messaging by:

Reach:
Estimated number of HCPs that a campaign can reach

Frequency:
Average number of messages displayed to an HCP

Share of voice:
Analysis of brand visibility compared to competitors in the market

Script lift:
Number of prescriptions written

Use of coupons & co-pay cards:
Amount of affordability payment options accepted

The distinction of messages needs to provide a one-to-one interaction that offers precise communications resonating with the target audience and to impart additional wisdom to their patients during consultations. The correlation of interactions to these necessary metrics in the point-of-care space provides clarity for the messages that are efficiently connecting with the target audience to achieve the desired outcomes.

In point-of-care channels, the reach of providers is massive with the platforms being an essential resource for HCPs to fulfill their professional responsibilities. Within these virtual mediums, brands have an opportunity to deliver non-invasive messages to when their target is the closest to caring and prescribing therapies to patients.

Having organizations support the education of clinicians will position marketers to better understand their needs and the content that is relevant for them. Further, point-of-care platforms are more performance oriented. Marketers can, thus, take more data-driven approaches for campaigns.

It's important to quantify communications efforts in today's point-of-care messaging landscape. Depending on the specialty, platform and demography of your target audience, the reach will vary for point-of-care campaigns. However, in preparation for aligning on messaging strategies, it's vital for companies to know the reach for the campaign to get the most out of the programs.

By calculating the reach, an organization can determine the proper allocation of resources and budget for the campaign to ensure an ample ROI is achieved. Organizations need to have an overview of the potential reach for a campaign to determine the value of proceeding with a campaign. Whether it's deploying messages in a telehealth or EHR platform, the opportunity to reach HCPs must be prevalent to attribute time and resources towards crafting a campaign. The reach is an estimated number of HCPs that can be targeted in a campaign.

With a vast overview of the target audience within the digital point-of-care ecosystem, marketers are able to control their communication plans to ensure their efforts are going to break through to their target audience. By having an opportunity to reach clinicians with the desired messaging, there are greater chances for marketers to achieve their business objectives.

After the reach has been established for the target audience, companies can shift their focus on the frequency of messages. As the campaign is taking place, it's important for marketers to know the frequency of the communications. By learning the average amount of time a message is being viewed by the targeted HCPs, brands can monitor how influential the content is that's being distributed.

Therefore, it's essential to equip marketers with a measurement platform that tracks the frequency of messages to ensure the interactions brands deploy to prescribers are resonating with them.

For point-of-care communications, marketers need to detect the frequency that's taking place throughout the online networks. As the metrics are being collected within the virtual mediums, brands are able to understand the types of platforms that their messages are appearing on. Therefore, if the exchanges aren't garnering the intended traction, marketers can closely examine if particular moments during the physician's journey are impacting the messaging efforts or if the platforms are experiencing differing results.

With data analytics available across online systems, the frequency of communications is monitored on individual platforms, which will dictate the mediums that are achieving more success in reaching the clinicians.

> Marketers shouldn't overlook share of voice.

For the share of voice metric, companies are able to become alert of brand awareness for their niche audience of HCPs in the life sciences sector. By gaining the data for this measurement, businesses can see the volume of conversations that are tied to their company within the industry. Simply, divide your brand's measurement figure by the amount of the total market to learn your company's share of voice in the space of point-of-care communications.

For some brands it will confirm dominance. However, others will notice a smaller market impact and can utilize the data to carve out a larger share of voice in the space. Thus, measuring the brand awareness across point-of-care systems is invaluable knowledge for a company to see how the organization stacks up against their competition. It's important to note that a company's share of voice tends to coincide with the market and revenue size of the businesses in the sector.

With the intelligence on a brand's share of voice, marketers gain a clear picture of the company's success with communications in the market. It provides them the opportunity to recognize areas to improve their power to better connect with HCPs. This can embolden brands to examine the current landscape and map their plans to achieve a greater share of the category.

> In addition, future campaigns can support brand management and address any new messaging elements that are needed to better educate audiences in the space. By learning the company's share of voice, marketers are able to gain audience-specific insights to segment HCPs for future interactions within point-of-care channels. It also offers a glimpse into what works for a competitor's campaign that can cultivate a new idea to drive brand initiatives.

Measure script lift to identify the impact of messages during an HCP's journey

Script lift is an increase in drugs prescribed by physicians to their patients. Marketers are apt to utilize technologies to boost this metric with the support of data analytics that can identify the messages and instances during an HCP's workflow that elevate the prescription being written for a patient.

The use of measurement solutions are formidable resources to gain data analytics that leads marketers to comprehend the point-of-care landscape to better deploy messages to providers when they are most receptive to prescribe a drug or a treatment to their patient. The POC is where patients are being treated, and thus it's critical to ultimately decipher if the communications are achieving the desired ROI for businesses.

Being able to monitor the usage of coupons and co-pay cards is valuable intel for point-of-care campaigns. Data analytics captured when patient affordability programs are being shared with HCPs as they are conversing with their patient raises awareness for when financial assistance is getting passed along to a patient. Further, when this metric is tracked, it enables organizations to identify the prescriptions that are being used to improve medication adherence.

In addition, the knowledge on the amount of patient assistance programs being utilized throughout the market will provide a company with more brand recognition that is being achieved during point-of-care projects. As organizations bring cost-saving measures to the forefront of virtual consultations by sharing messages about the availability of co-pay cards and coupons for a prescribed drug, patients are more likely to take the medication as recommended, since the monetary cost of the therapy isn't' a hardship on the person.

Also, the measurement of patient assistance programs being shared with prescriptions provides additional data sets on an HCP's prescribing behavior, which will enable future communications to be tailored to their treatment practices.

When vanity metrics are being used, the outcomes may be misrepresented to an organization that has their marketing philosophy misinformed for current and future initiatives. If a campaign doesn't position a brand towards these sought-after metrics that support the company, the organization needs to reassess their measurement approach for campaigns. Data analytics from the aforementioned areas are pivotal instead of vanity metrics to provide a thorough overview of messaging projects to optimize efforts.

Mark Brosso
Founder & CEO at PurpleLab, LLC

My wife and friends frequently ask me "why do I see pharma ads everywhere I look?" and I tell them, an ad-buy's the cheapest part of the process and the ROI is proven. That makes it make sense to purchase, even if you're seeing the same ad on your smart TV twice in ten minutes. What's smarter than that is the ability to ferret out that second ad and stop paying for it. That's where Doceree's measurement enters the picture.

There's a cyclical relationship between advancements in ad serving and measurement technology. We've seen several iterations of this in the past — on the open web, the growth of viewability, and increasingly on CTV, with frequency capping. Put bluntly, the ability to advertise runs way out ahead of the ability to tell what works, and a lot of ad dollars go to waste in that gap. Healthcare marketing in particular, has gone through this with the development of digital point-of-care advertising. Brand awareness, education, and market access initiatives like couponing all depend on reaching their audience at the right time in the care pathway. The messaging that someone needs at a primary care practice can be very different from what is relevant in a specialty practice where a physician is evaluating competing brands for an indication, and the only way to tease that out is through the rigorous, machine learning powered testing Harshit Jain has developed in Doceree. This book helps outline what the metrics are that marketers need to account for in their POC campaigns to optimize for success.

06

POINT-OF-CARE MESSAGING MYTHS

There are myths associated with POC messaging that are misinterpreted by organizations. When life sciences brands explore introducing point-of-care channels into their messaging repertoire, it's crucial that the misconceptions about practices with point-of-care communications be understood. I'll address those areas that may have led to uncertainties and confusion for players to enter the market and set aside hesitations so that marketers are well-versed about the truth behind the myths in the space.

As a physician, I am aware that fabrications can prohibit growth and exploration in a burgeoning market.

MYTH	**FACT**
Messaging within EHR platforms is not compliant with pharmaceutical laws	Messaging within EHR platforms presents options, but the decisions rest with the physician

Organizations in the life sciences category need to establish their ethical boundaries and not faulter when it comes to establishing the policies for communication plans. With point-of-care communications, there's a perception that messages being served to HCPs are influencing the drugs and therapies that physicians are prescribing to their patients. However, the views about interactions by life sciences companies with prescribers within EHR systems not being compliant with pharmaceutical laws are a fallacy.

The lapse in knowledge about the policies of messaging in EHR systems has led marketers to have hesitancy in implementing communication strategies in the digital workflow of clinicians. While communications are delivered to physicians during their clinical workflow, the messages being served are permitted to support prescribers with educational resources.

This is a common practice that empowers brands to share informative materials that are compliant with industry regulations. With messages being facilitated within EHR platforms, providers are equipped with additional knowledge pertaining to their specialty that ensure their awareness of the latest developments in their medical field.

By adhering to these practices, marketers put the prescribing decisions in the hands of the clinician. The educational content being delivered under the industry guidelines enables more informative dialogue to be fostered during consultations, so physicians can make well-informed decisions to treat their patients.

MYTH	FACT
Engagement is less on point-of-care platforms than traditional marketing channels	Engagement isn't a metric that marketers should seek to achieve with point-of-care messaging campaigns

Interactions with HCPs on digital point-of-care platforms are designed to reach clinicians when they are closest to their patients. Therefore, click-through rates aren't an advisable metric, since messages are designed to inform HCPs in a seamless manner that doesn't take them to another digital medium. With these virtual exchanges, marketers don't want to seek engagement because the communications are meant to keep the attention on their patients. Further, the content shared is crafted to keep prescribers within the platform while being engaged with their patients instead of taking them to another online channel.

With engagement not being part of a company's scope for campaigns, metrics such as reach, frequency, share of voice, script lift and the use of co-pay cards and coupons are the data analytics that are monitored for messaging initiatives to comprehend the business objectives that are achieved. Marketers need to eliminate the measurement of engagement in EHRs to ensure a clinician's EHR experience isn't disrupted.

Actions are sought-after by marketers, but a click for engagement is not a necessary outcome for point- of-care communications. The action of absorbing a message to treat their patient or retain the message to explore the drug or research study after tending to the person is the beneficial action for meaningful results in the virtual point-of-care ecosystem.

MYTH	FACT
Telehealth platforms are only used for messaging to patients	Life sciences organizations use telehealth platforms to message HCPs and patients

The experience within telehealth platforms varies for HCPs and patients. Therefore, the communications that are distributed within telehealth channels target clinicians and patients separately. A consumer-centric message won't be visible to providers and vice versa. Marketers differentiate their approach when interacting with clinicians and patients, since the knowledge base of providers is stronger within their respective medical field.

Each person has their own digital journey during telehealth consultations. Marketers can tailor communications to the target audience based on the data analytics obtained to understand the interests of the intended recipient. A focal point of achieving better health outcomes is the common factor of interactions with prescribers and patients.

For interactions with HCPs within telehealth networks, marketers comprehend the stages of the discussions that take place with an individual. Therefore, organizations strategically deploy messages to providers to reflect the current moment of the telehealth visit to ensure the content is supportive to the clinician to diagnose and prescribe a therapy to the person.

MYTH
It's not possible to reach physicians at the point-of-care who use Epic and Cerner EHR systems

FACT
Physicians can be reached via apps within Epic's App Orchard and Cerner's Open Developer Program

Epic and Cerner operate leading EHR systems and have developer programs named App Orchard and Cerner's Open Developer Experience (code), respectively. The digital health ecosystem being run by the companies doesn't prohibit organizations from working with firms having platforms in each of the company's app store. So, the notion that brands can't reach physicians utilizing EHR networks within an Epic or Cerner system is fictitious.

While the businesses behind the large hospital EHR systems may not permit messaging to physicians within their own channel, the opportunity to connect with HCPs within the apps listed in each company's app stores persists. The comprehension of how the apps structure in association with each business enables marketers to have the wherewithal to facilitate campaigns to reach HCPs within the Epic and Cerner networks.

Fig 4: Selection of apps in Epic App Orchard

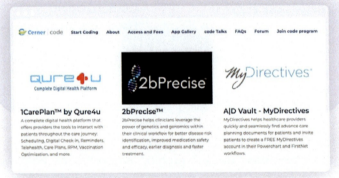

Fig 5: Selection of apps in Cerner Open Developer Experience (code)

MYTH

Geotargeted advertising to physicians in hospitals is the same as point-of-care messaging

FACT

Targeting physician in a hospital within point-of-care platforms is account-based marketing

The strategy of marketers set out to connect with target audiences and reach physicians in hospitals within the online point-of-care spectrum is more precise than geotargeting ads to prescribers within the medical facility. Knowing the location of a provider inside of the hospital doesn't deliver the customization that's necessary to understand the prescribing behaviors, communication preferences and educational needs of an HCP that's necessary for an effective point-of-care campaign.

Also, geo-targeting physicians fails to establish the specialty of the provider being targeted to deploy messages that are of relevance to their medical profession and can assist with the care of their patients. Furthermore, physicians use non-professional sites and platforms within the hospital that doesn't reach them during their moments of care delivery.

When marketers set out to target physicians within hospitals at the point-of-care, then it is referred to as account-based marketing and reaches prescribers while they are checking on their patients and conducting professional responsibilities. This approach enables organizations to personalize communications to HCPs that reflect their behaviors and practices within digital point-of-care channels. The individualization of messages that are shared during account-based marketing efforts ensures that the content is of interest to the target audience and aligns with their specialty.

07

ADHERE TO INDUSTRY REGULATIONS FOR
POINT-OF-CARE MESSAGING

The Health Insurance Portability and Accountability Act of 1996 (HIPAA) is commonly thought of when discussing messaging at the point-of-care. However, in the case of life sciences brands targeting HCPs, HIPAA doesn't apply to this target audience, as the policy was established to protect the sensitive health information of patients. With HIPAA, electronic protected health information (ePHI) covered any materials that were stored, transmitted, received, or utilized within an electronic platform from unauthorized parties.

Nonetheless, marketers do have industry guidelines that companies must adhere to when targeting HCPs at the POC. The acceleration of digital mediums by prescribers and patients during the pandemic will introduce updated regulations into the market to address the changing digital environment for medical professionals.

With the prominence of virtual care, legislations will continue to progress to ensure policies are established to recognize the technological developments that have entered the market since previous regulations were enacted.

Data privacy remains an emphasis for the development of laws and policies to reflect the broad adoption of virtual care channels. Marketers must navigate HIPAA to maintain the anonymity of individuals that receive care from clinicians while delivering precise messages to HCPs based on their specialty and prescribing behaviors.

Life sciences brands utilize first-party data to identify and target prescribers. Further, companies that align with partners to obtain audience identifiers are an additional resource for marketers to reach their target audience while adhering to industry regulations.

First-party data is an asset for marketing campaigns because it's data that is collected directly for an individual, and so marketers can trust that the information is accurate when targeting audiences for a campaign. Thus, to accumulate this data, it's necessary for businesses to gain consent from the person to obtain and use their provided information for marketing purposes. Therefore, the company has control on how the data is used and is responsible for its security to maintain the trust of the user that provided their information based on the stated intentions for gathering the data.

Companies must explain why and how the data is being collected to the user. By providing a simple explanation about the usage of an HCP's data, an individual can decide to opt-in and provide personal data to the organization. This practice supports businesses to be transparent with clinicians when obtaining first-party data.

With the California Consumer Privacy Act (CCPA) and European Union's General Data Protection Regulation (GDPR), already in place for the respective regions, more data privacy laws will fall under the scope of life sciences marketers and platforms to understand and conform their marketing practices around.

While communications are taking place across online channels, it's crucial for personal identifiers and protected health information (PHI) to be anonymized to deploy campaigns to providers. This empowers marketers to deliver precise messages to their target audience while still protecting their health information.

A patient's privacy is essential for messaging campaigns, so businesses must have in place proper policies and protocols to ensure data protection is taking place when gathering data sets on HCPs to enrich communication efforts.

> The introduction of the **Health Information Technology for Economic and Clinical Health (HITECH) Act** led to the compliance of HIPPA guidelines by companies. That they were ensuring health information was kept confidential. In case guidelines were not followed, substantial fines were imposed. With the HITECH Act, businesses had to be compliant with HIPAA security and privacy rules.

With the rise of virtual care during the Covid-19, the mandates for eRx to be offered to patients have taken effect in most states in the United States. The importance of effectively targeting clinicians within eRx channels will be pivotal as legislations further entrench these virtual mediums as part of the online healthcare system.

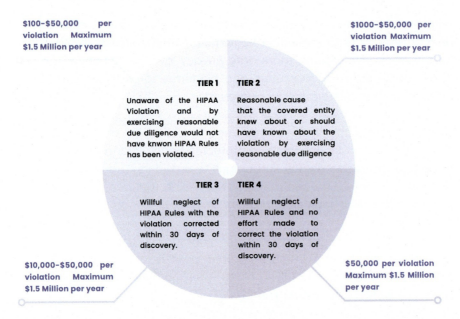

Fig 6: HIPAA violation penalties

With the rapid evolution of the point-of-care category, marketers must remain diligent in learning about the introduction of new regulations that companies must adhere to when interacting with HCPs.

With the acceleration of the digital ecosystem for marketers to communicate with HCPs, the policies put in place to protect the health data between patients and providers under HIPAA in 1990 are being revisited to modernize regulations on the collection of health data by organizations. As virtual health technologies advance the category, new policies will be introduced to govern the way technologies are utilized within the sector.

Where is e-prescrepting required by law?
A Centers for Medicare & Medicaid Services (CMS) rule requiring that Part D providers EPCS took effect January 1, 2021 (pursuant to the requirements of the SUPPORT for Patients and Communities Act), and state legislation continued moving forward throughout the year,

3 states passed mandates in 2021.

14 states had manadtes take effect during 2021.

6 states had manadtes take effect on Jan 1, 2022.

35 states have now passed e-prescribing mandates.

75% of U.S. population lives in states with mandates in effect.

32 states have mandates in effect as of Jan 2021.

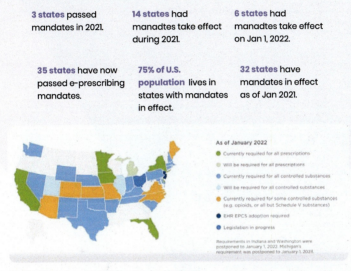

Fig 7: Where is e-prescribing required by law?

08

A GLOBAL PERSPECTIVE ON THE POINT-OF-CARE MESSAGING LANDSCAPE

While point-of-care messaging is now prevalent around the world, the initiatives must adhere to the policies and standards while deploying messages to reach HCPs. The communications that take place within POC networks vary, so it's essential to devise online campaigns that are suitable for the country they are being facilitated in.

While the communication strategies to connect with providers progress in emerging markets, organizations have to understand the habits and preferences of physicians to penetrate international markets with point-of-care messaging plans that local prescribers being targeted can relate to.

Being able to develop a spectrum of digital messaging programs that will effectively reach HCPs in various areas can uplift a brand's traction in a region. The construction of communication initiatives can lead organizations to devise an approach to gain traction with providers. When calculating methods to reach an HCP virtually at the point-of-care, marketers identifying the digital channels that are most used in the international market can optimize the impact of messaging efforts for the company.

In 2021, North America had the largest revenue share (45.4%) in the $27.2 billion global EHR market.[32] The usage of the online medium is progressing worldwide, but additional platforms are being utilized at the point-of-care in global markets that can elevate the messaging initiatives being conducted.

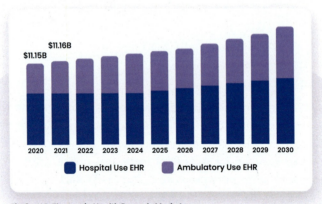

Fig 8: U.S. Electronic Health Records Market

As the EHR category grows, more countries are becoming accustomed to point-of-care platforms, and how messages can be tailored to the specialty of the provider to enrich their virtual care sessions with patients.

> The distribution of informative messages that help HCPs in their medical field will lead caregivers to embrace digital interactions with brands in more international markets.

WhatsApp's role in real-time interactions

With a plethora of EHR, telehealth and eRx platforms utilized in the United States by HCPs, WhatsApp is a medium that's not relied upon in the healthcare setting in the country but is of significance in other international regions. The usage of WhatsApp has been adopted by clinicians in international markets to better communicate with patients.

The use of WhatsApp opens a forum for improved communications with physicians by having the ability to interact with their patients in a more immediate capacity. The effectiveness of interactions being held more promptly is constructive when marketers serve messages to providers that are beneficial to treating a patient. A perception of instantaneous responses can be disadvantageous for prescribers to balance their workload and can deteriorate the HCP-patient relationship if there is a disparity in the sense of urgency following a message being sent from a patient to their clinician. The progression of virtual solutions in the space enables WhatsApp to be a helpful tool to engage with patients who heavily use the app.

As Asia-Pacific markets shift to digital solutions from in-person operations with clinicians, marketers within these regions have to adapt to messaging tactics to evolve with the online behaviors of caregivers.

As part of the challenges, the use of online mediums is recognized in the case of WhatsApp and protecting the patient's data and overcoming the lack of documentation in an individual's medical records. The use of WhatsApp in Europe requires organizations to comply with GDPR to protect the patient's information.

Meanwhile, the pandemic led to an increase in telemedicine consultations, which boosted the use of WhatsApp in the healthcare landscape. In addition, virtual interactions are taking place in WhatsApp around requests for prescriptions and medical reports and verifying information as caregivers tend to a patient.

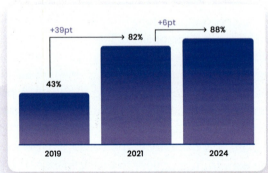

Fig 9: Telemedicine adoption among physicians -40pt from 2019

In China, the adoption rate of hospital EHRs increased from 18.6% in 2007 to 85.3% in 2018. For comparison, the adoption rate went from 9.4% to 96% for hospitals in the US during that period.[33] The digital systems are progressing throughout Asia with the EHR adoption rate having increased from 15.1% in 2010 to 58.1% in 2015 in Korean hospitals and from 21% in 2008 to 53% in 2014 in Japanese public hospitals.[34] EHR systems are more prevalent in Europe as well and the usage of EHRs in German hospitals rose from 39.9% in 2007 to 68.4% in 2017.[35]

The integration of EHR systems in Asia has become a viable solution for providers to monitor for diseases and predict high-risk areas. Consequently, the infrastructure is progressing in the emerging markets to offer virtual health systems to improve the quality of care for patients. As the online practices present a challenge to connect with prescribers, marketers have to refine communication efforts to deliver messages that the target audience relates to breakthrough to support HCPs during virtual care activities.

Rank	Australia	China	India	Indonesia	Singapore	Malaysia	Philippines
1	Primary care providers 73%	Secondary/tertiary care providers 82%	Pharmacies 73%	Health insurers 74%	Primary care providers 74%	Secondary/tertiary care providers 71%	Pharmacies 70%
2	Secondary/tertiary care providers 68%	The government 82%	Secondary/tertiary care providers 72%	Pharmacies 72%	Secondary/tertiary care providers 73%	Primary care providers 69%	Primary care providers 66%
3	Pharmacies 63%	Primary care providers 67%	Primary care providers 71%	Secondary/tertiary care providers 71%	The government 68%	Pharmacies 61%	Pharmaceutical companies 63%
	Technology companies 21% (9)	Technology companies 59% (5)	Technology companies 69% (6)	Technology companies 65% (5)	Technology companies 45% (7)	Technology companies 40% (9)	Technology companies 44% (9)

Improvement in rank compared with 2019   Decline in rank compared with 2019   No change in rank compared with 2019

Question: How much would you trust the following to manage your overall healthcare and coordinate your treatments with other healthcare providers in your country?
Notes: For India, trust in general insurers and trust in the government were recorded together; percent of respondents include those who responded "Somewhat Trust" or "Completely Trust"; Malaysia and Philippines were not included in the 2019 survey, hence past rank comparison is not available for these two countries; "pharmacies" was also added to the 2020 survey so comparison with 2019 data is not available for this option.
Source: Bain Front Line of Healthcare Asia-Pacific Survey, 2021 (n=1,750), 2019 (n=1,521)

Fig 10: Patients trust care providers and pharmacies most, but are gaining confidence in tech companies

Europe is a competitive market for digital solutions in the point-of-care category. Large vendors such as Epic, Cerner and Allscripts are leading the industry with a strong position in multiple regions in Europe, but smaller companies are also having success in the continent.[36] To facilitate campaigns to reach clinicians in Europe, marketers need to turn to GDPR-compliant solutions that empower their organizations to adhere to the latest regulations when targeting clinicians across the region.

Point-of-care messaging is the future of messaging campaigns targeting HCPs worldwide. As the use of EHR systems expands globally, the importance of communicating seamlessly during the provider's workflow is instrumental to boost the ROI for messaging efforts.

The execution of point-of-care communications in the United States serves as a guide for how marketers universally can embrace online mediums to improve communications with prescribers. By capturing data points about the practicing behaviors and prescribing habits of clinicians, marketers can pinpoint the moments of an HCP's digital journey that are opportune to deliver messages to HCPs.

By having the ability to see how the messaging initiatives evolved via digital campaigns that were formulated at the POC, companies in the global markets can refine approaches to effectively reach HCPs while they are in a professional mindset. The procedures that have proved successful in the US can be adapted to efficiently reach HCPs at the point-of-care worldwide.

09

WHAT LIFE SCIENCES BRANDS NEED TO KNOW ABOUT HCP COMMUNICATIONS

The embrace of digital technologies is progressing within the life sciences industry as 81% of healthcare business leaders have reported their organization is accelerating digital use in 2021, and 93% conveyed that their organizations are innovating with a sense of urgency and call to action.[37]

Since marketers have shifted from antiquated point-of-care marketing methods, digital communications have the power to enrich the dialogue between physicians and their patients. When life sciences brands cultivate communication plans to reach clinicians, trust needs to be at the forefront as strategies are executed. Companies have to build trust for the messages that are deployed to HCPs, which in turn must be relevant for the providers to have the confidence to share those learnings with their patients to adhere to the advised therapy.

The trust philosophy may seem simple but accomplishing it is no easy feat. A marketer needs to deliver integrity during communication initiatives with conviction. Further, the targeted clinicians need the mentality to welcome messages to assist with their education to foster a meaningful and lasting connection with a brand. As digital technologies revolutionize the way POC campaigns are devised, operated and viewed, the innovations can expound the strategies that elevate the outcomes of communications.

Implementing point-of-care messaging strategies

Organizations must have an outlook on point-of-care communications that's digital-first. As marketers transition to emphasize online elements to reach physicians, they have to adjust their vision for campaigns in the digital realm instead of being focused on physical materials within a medical facility. Further, when implementing a strategy to connect with prescribers, marketers need to reflect on what HCPs need and what is the optimal way to reach the targeted prescriber. Once those areas are established, planning can begin to ensure that messaging efforts are on the most favorable path to benefit the company.

Now, preparation with the support of data analytics can begin to take shape. Though, I'd be remiss if I didn't take this moment to emphasize the importance of monitoring the market. The digital point-of-care space is in the early stages of development and thus the category is evolving as new solutions continue to enrich the experience within point-of-care platforms for clinicians and their patients.

For marketers, the plans must be based on data analytics. With a plethora of metrics available, marketers can begin to identify the cohorts of physicians to initiate the process to arrive at personalized content that will resonate with the target audience. As companies begin to formulate the profiles of target audiences, marketers have the ability to prepare messages that reflect the interests of the providers.

> Embrace data-based learnings from metrics to customize messages to an HCP's specialty that will resonate with them during their workflow.

To maximize the value of the messages, the content needs to be appropriate to the platform it's being shared on. So, training marketers to understand the facets of the point-of-care networks is crucial to grasp how physicians are utilizing the channels. Marketers then know how and when the messages are poised to garner the greatest impact. Getting down to the intricacies of EHRs, telehealth, eRx and the additional systems are instrumental in knowing how marketers can elevate each medium to better support physicians during their time within the online ecosystem. I'll delve into more specifics pertaining to each type of channels later in the book.

As I mentioned, metrics are crucial to have a point-of-care campaign thrive. So, when the communications are up and running, marketers must track the results. A measurement tool becomes a valuable asset for businesses to examine the outcomes of messages being deployed. The digital skillset of marketers is worth emphasizing to ensure that their time is spent effectively, and data points aren't missed within the platform.

And of course, following the implementation of strategies, marketers should experiment by testing various formats and terminology for the messages and the moments within point-of-care channels when the content is distributed to collect the metrics via a measurement platform to ensure the best path toward the desired audience is being attained.

As online communications advance in the sector, companies can continue to analyze and learn from the messaging practices that were put in place and ensure those procedures are being optimized with the current behaviors of physicians during their journey across the digital ecosystem.

> Any messaging that we as a physician see should not only be about the drug and its composition, but it should go beyond. The messaging should be able to convey clearly how it will help physicians in their practice and how it can benefit their patients. That's what physicians are eventually interested in – anything with which they can serve their patients better and something that improves their practice.

Benefits of virtual messaging campaigns for HCPs

Communications held within digital point-of-care networks offer brands the opportunity to reach HCPs during decision-making moments. Being able to navigate the online journey of physicians is challenging for marketers, but the implementation of the approaches that I've just detailed, and the interactions distributed within the channels are advantageous for companies to become trusted resources for clinicians.

When prescribers are active on POC platforms, organizations can facilitate messages that support the care a clinician is able to provide to their patients. With the knowledge of a provider's specialty, marketers can narrow down the focus of the exchanges with the HCPs to elevate their expertise in their medical field.

Whether it's a new drug entering the market or a research study about therapies, HCPs are tasked with being updated as patients trust their care provider to be aware of the latest practices and treatments. When brands have the wisdom on what their target audience needs to better tend to their patients, better health outcomes will be achieved.

By being engaged with patients during their virtual consultations, marketers can connect with providers while they have an active dialogue with individuals. The brands that prioritize high-quality content that expands the HCP's familiarity in their profession is well-received by prescribers as those online exchanges improve their practicing routines to care for their patients.

The significance of personized communications

When marketers don't seek out data analytics to identify the appropriate audience to deliver content to, the messages are going to fall flat and not gain meaningful exchanges. Therefore, when content is being crafted for point-of-care campaigns, the message must be customized to reflect the exact medical field that the provider practices. Communications for a primary care physician is going to vary for an oncologist. So, the precision of messages is fundamental to setting a strong foundation for the deployment of a campaign.

As HCPs navigate digital point-of-care systems, personalized messages showcase that the brand understands the prescriber's needs to get on their radar. Even if the initial messages don't achieve the desired outcomes for a brand, the communications being on point with the provider's current circumstances will curry favor for future interactions. Consequently, the relationship is being nurtured as forthcoming messages continue to demonstrate that the company recognizes the provider's areas of need.

The power to address a subject that is in demand by the physician affords them to minimize their time between visits or after work hours to find and learn about a patient's ailments and to help them recover or discover the latest therapy that's beneficial to advise a patient about. The more in-depth specifics marketers can learn about a clinician, the more individualized the content can be made to their practices and procedures they follow.

Make campaigns more efficient

With HCPs embracing online mediums, marketers in the industry followed suit to reach prescribers across virtual point-of-care platforms. With the transition to digital initiatives, it opened the opportunity for marketers to gain more data analytics on their target audience to institute more efficient messaging operations.

> Therefore, it's necessary for brands to invest in the solutions to guide the direction of messaging efforts. The learnings obtained from the data sets amassed on the target audiences and metrics for the results on the distributed messages embolden organizations to examine the highs and the lows of their programs. These particular datapoints are highly beneficial when implementing trigger-based messaging campaigns to narrow down the instances during an HCPs journey when monetary resources should be allocated for specific segments and channels that achieve a superior business outcome.

Decipher the opportune moments to deploy trigger-based messages to clinicians.

Data must be compiled and analyzed to uncover the areas where the messaging is providing the highest ROI for the desired business outcomes. As data sets are accumulated, marketers are afforded the metrics that embolden their strategies with the data-based approach. The actionable insights garnered from prior communications enable marketers to put forth calculated communication efforts to realize the path forward to alter budgets away from low-performing aspects of campaigns to more high-performing elements to achieve the awareness desired via communications to HCPs.

Being equipped with a comprehensive understanding of the physician predicates the success that's to come for communications within point-of-care channels. By operating with a data-centric mindset, the strategies progress based on trends that are deciphered during messaging efforts in the online ecosystem. The learnings of past campaigns need to be incorporated to optimize approaches to reach HCPs in an efficient manner.

Embrace data transparency for campaign results

To operate efficient messaging campaigns, organizations need data transparency to be able to embrace actionable insights to remove ambiguity from POC campaigns. By having transparency for the results of communications, marketers are afforded the opportunity to refine tactics to achieve their desired outcomes. When the metrics for the communications are attainable in real-time, marketing budgets can be shifted to optimize the spending for messaging placements.

> With the digital tools available for marketers to be aware of high-performing as well as low-performing elements of campaigns, those data-based insights can better prepare brands to reach prescribers optimally. The status quo of reaching HCPs doesn't consist of deploying messages and letting the campaign run its course. By gaining metrics on the performance of the campaign, marketers are primed with the resources to alter strategies when necessary to optimize communications to providers.

When data transparency isn't provided, marketers may have a false sense of the achievements being gained throughout the duration of a campaign. Ultimately, if the business outcomes aren't accomplished at the conclusion of the campaign, then it's too late for organizations to make adjustments to their messages being deployed and the point-of-care channels that are being leveraged to reach clinicians.

The ability to associate particular point-of-care platforms and messages with results is a monumental asset for marketers to pinpoint the content and its location during a physician's workflow that is garnering the greatest impact. With transparency provided throughout communications in the digital ecosystem, organizations in the life sciences industry are afforded an all-encompassing assessment of interactions to boost the ROI of the campaigns.

With the use of data analytics in a transparent manner, the category will prosper by knowing the messages that are being valued by HCPs and the method that is preferred by target audiences to receive interactions from brands. The ability to make data-based decisions enables marketers to elevate the value of communications for brands, but also deliver more purposeful messaging to prescribers across point-of-care systems.

The value of HCP communications

A report discovered that a quarter of HCPs believe pharma companies could do more to understand digital communications.[38] In addition, the study revealed that 86% of HCPs found content that goes beyond product information from pharma companies to be truly helpful.[39] So, marketers are aware of the value that is presented to clinicians at the point-of-care to improve the cognizance of industry developments with caregivers via messaging that keeps them apprised of current professional information in their medical field.

At the POC, organizations have an avenue open to interact with prescribers, and how those messages are further shared during their conversations with their patient.

When businesses focus on boosting script lift via branded messages within point-of-care networks, the opportunity arises to expand the education of the market. As marketers target providers who stand to benefit from learning about a drug or treatment to consider prescribing it to their patients, those messages have a direct correlation to the company's bottom line.

However, unbranded campaigns must not be forgotten as an effective way to aid physicians and encourage their education about research conducted on treatments. While an organization may not receive the immediate prescription of their drug, the informative content will raise awareness within the target clinician's specialty. With the expanded acumen of the provider, their dialogue is enriched during consultations with patients to empower them to arrive at the therapy that is ideal for the treated individual.

Also, when branded messages are distributed during a separate campaign, the brand unlocks the possibility to generate more revenue with the broad messaging having already left an impression on the prescriber as they diagnose and treat their patients.

Ritesh Patel
Sr. Partner, Global Digital Health at FINN Partners

It is now a well-known fact that the Pandemic has forced many industries to re-evaluate how they market, sell, and engage with their customers. We now live on our mobiles as we buy more from ads on social media and expect things to be delivered to us at the press of a button. This new environment has created many opportunities to rethink business models, marketing, and communications.

The healthcare industry has not been immune to this new world. In 2020, marketers quickly accelerated the use of digital technologies with almost the entire life sciences and biotech industry adopting "Veeva Rep Triggered Emails" as the new communications and sales tool. But that still relied on the reps. Fast forward to 2022, the life sciences industry is coming to terms with this new world and the words "Omnichannel strategy/Roadmap/ capability" are permeating throughout. Dr. Jain outlines a solid framework for this new digital ecosystem we are entering into:

Data: Collecting and using data to inform all of your activities

Experience: Defining and designing an optimal customer experience across channels and platforms

Channels: Engagement on the right platform at the right time

Content: Creating relevant, contextual and engaging content

Technology: Tools for managing the engagement

This new model he outlines should be the blueprint for all life sciences marketers for HCP engagement in the future.

10

UNDERSTANDING THE DIGITAL WORKFLOW OF HCPs

The digital journey of HCPs is complex and takes marketers on a whirlwind through online mediums such as telehealth, eRx and EHR systems. Marketers have a significant task to navigate these virtual channels to reach physicians with messages while their target audience is conducting one of the countless tasks that are applicable to point-of-care platforms.

Whether clinicians are consulting a patient in real-time or reviewing a person's medical history, marketers have to decipher the sequences that make up a provider's workflow to identify the occasions for when communications are going to effectively reach the prescriber. The digital portals continue to evolve for physicians as virtual care becomes a prominent offering in the category. So, marketers must adapt to the way caregivers are tending to their patients, receiving lab results, and tracking an individual's health progress to refine tactics for when messages should be displayed within POC platforms.

To really know the intricacies of the way online channels are being utilized by an HCP during their day, marketers need to understand a platform to capture data analytics to gain actionable insights. Research has shown that HCPs spend up to five hours for every eight hours of scheduled clinical time using EHR systems.[40] Further, prescribers' time using those digital mediums extends to an average of 1.4 additional hours outside of clinical work hours.[41]

With all the time spent within EHR systems alone, marketers that are armed with data points on their target audience can prepare the facilitation of campaigns by obtaining the behaviors and preferences of providers to deliver more personalized communications. However, companies have to comprehend the entire breadth of the HCP's digital journey to formulate a plan for the delivery of messages to their target audience.

Digital messages must be shared in a seamless manner to support the provider's workflow.

Now let's look at what a typical day in the life of a physician may look like. While drinking their morning coffee before arriving at the office, clinicians are connected to their devices with a wide range of activities that span personal and professional interests such as reading their personal and work emails, checking their social media accounts, reading news and visiting professional websites to get familiar with any recent industry update.

Upon entering the office, providers begin their workday with the continuation of research on online medical journals and medical association websites. In addition, they're monitoring communications and records within eRx and EHR platforms before their first patient visit commences in a telehealth channel. As clinicians meet with patients throughout the day, they're regularly connected to the digital point-of-care ecosystem while charting and prescribing medications.

Even during lunch and evening hours, physicians can be found on their smartphones, tablets or laptops accessing point-of-care mediums to complete a patient's chart or read about studies to arrive at a diagnosis and treatment for their patients. The workflow of HCPs is connected across devices and creates an opportunity for marketers to identify their habits to learn when the distribution of messages will best serve them and their patients.

Hence, HCPs are open to communications in POC networks more frequently compared to their time spent on endemic and non-endemic channels. Furthermore, the use of point-of-care platforms elevates contextual messaging that will be displayed to prescribers.

With physicians navigating POC channels throughout their digital workflow, marketers are poised to serve messages that are relevant to their medical field as they meet with their patients. While clinicians are active throughout the day on online point-of-care platforms, they are also in the medical mindset while engaging with these virtual mediums. Brands need to focus on connecting with prescribers while they are tending to their patients and can benefit from additional educational materials to learn more about medical conditions and treatments to make informed decisions for their patients

> Meanwhile, outside of office hours when a physician may be reading online news publications or checking their social media accounts, having messages displayed then have the possibility of being overlooked with their mental focus on personal interests.

So, it's imperative for the communications to be relative to their medical interests. As an HCP is researching a study in a medical journal during their lunch break while it's out of their point-of-care ecosystem, the exchange can still be relevant. The delivery of POC messages needs to be carefully monitored to ensure the content is being displayed in a relevant manner. An online visit from a medical journal to YouTube can drastically alter the type of messages that are timely to serve during their online journey outside of point-of-care systems.

This remains true after work when the contextual relevance of the materials being viewed online must pertain to a physician's medical field. Connecting with an HCP while the individual is checking their EHR after work hours remains to be relevant to their workflow that spans beyond the traditional office hours. Yet, if the physician opens a streaming service to watch a film, the subject becomes off- topic and the messages won't hold the same relevance for the intended audience.

During office hours, clinicians will remain connected with EHR, telehealth and eRx networks, but in what capacity are the caregivers using the online platforms? The comprehension of a physician's workflow is fundamental to efficiently interact with HCPs during campaigns. By spotting behavioral patterns and communication preferences across the multitude of point-of-care platforms, these learnings can guide messaging efforts to be cognizant of the channels that are more frequently visited.

> I reminisce that when I used to practice as a physician, I considered myself two personalities. In the role of a physician, I was treating and caring for my patients. In that zone, I wanted to learn more about drugs and therapies so I could continue to help my patients in the best way possible. The second personality was in which I was a fun-loving professional with a wife and a kid. In that zone, I thought of what we could do together and how could we have more family time. I always kept the two sides of me separate and didn't mix either of them. I knew if there was an overlap, I could not justify either. So, when I was scrolling through my Facebook page, that was my personal side and when I was checking Medscape, I was doing so professionally to gather information to serve my patients better.

Data analytics hold the key to meaningful exchanges

In addition, data analytics can embolden communication efforts by connecting the behaviors and actions within point-of-care systems and the reception that was received from messages being displayed in particular platforms, along with the moment during their workflow when the exchange was held.

Being able to track the prescriptions and therapies that follow the interactions is key for marketers to know the shared materials are beneficial for the clinician during the consultation with their patients. By knowing the communication patterns that are welcomed by physicians, organizations are more prepared to facilitate future messages to the prescriber in their preferred manner.

With the determination of the point-of-care platforms that a physician is using and how the usage of channels correlates to their interaction with the patient, AI-powered solutions can analyze and instruct marketers on the impact of digital exchanges.

> Identifying and comprehending the behavior patterns of providers will elevate the digital interactions being held with caregivers.

If an HCP is more receptive to communications within EHR systems, marketers can align the brand's strategies to distribute messages within an EHR as opposed to a telehealth network. Further, the use of data analytics can instruct an organization on the type of format and juncture of their workday or interaction with a patient that garners superior ROI.

The ability to tailor messages to reflect the habits of providers within point-of-care networks permits marketers to create a more meaningful experience for them. Whether it's a branded or unbranded campaign, when dealing with communications at the point-of-care, educational materials are essential to be shared with the caregiver.

Regardless of how well a brand can decipher the prime path to its target audience, the messages must be non-intrusive and educational. After all, HCPs want to maintain their knowledge in their specialty to ensure their patients are being treated properly. The cadence of informative communications that stoke the interest of the provider can swell the trust between a brand and its target audience.

Campaigns need to be comprised of contextual relevant messages that demonstrate an understanding of the provider's background and the mindset for the types of drugs and therapies that will be of interest when treating their patients. To facilitate those messaging efforts, the ability to capture data on the previously prescribed treatments guides marketers to distribute educational assets that are valuable to physicians for them to better advise and treat patients.

Point-of-care communications are reflective of where prescribers are spending most of their day, so the most meaningful interactions are messages that perfectly align with the approach an HCP takes with their patients and at the precise occurrence of their digital journey. As the bond between brands and providers is strengthened, additional contextual messages can be positioned throughout the clinician's workflow when the communications are most helpful.

Another important aspect of having communications served to prescribers is to not have the distribution of messages disrupt the HCP's journey. During their workflow, the patient is the main priority of caregivers. Therefore, marketers must respect that aspect of point-of-care communication efforts and not display messages that are intrusive to ensure that the physician-patient dialogue remains uninterrupted. The ability to facilitate informative messages that don't interfere with the conversations being held during the patient's visit is pivotal to the success of programs.

Further, an essential aspect of digital exchanges is to not disturb HCPs during their conversations with patients and not have the communication instruct prescribers to take an action, such as clicking on the message. In the physician's workflow, the engagement must remain between the physician and their patients and not measuring click-through rates to determine the impact of the campaigns.

When programmatic messaging capabilities are integrated with point-of-care messaging efforts, then automated communications can be distributed to optimize interactions during an HCP's workflow. Trigger-based messages are served via this programmatic method that aligns prescribers with messages that pertain to their current stage at the POC.

> The availability of data-based analytics provides the direction to virtual communications, empowering marketers to acknowledge the occurrences during a clinician's workflow when the content would help the provider to better instruct their patient about therapy options. The enhanced communications raise the value that marketers can deliver to HCPs and have meaningful interactions within point-of-care platforms in the process.

Communications in point-of-care platforms must be crafted to be an extension of the brand. So, use all resources to gain an all-inclusive perspective of an HCP's workflow to enrich their experience within the channels to showcase the brand's value to clinicians at the point-of-care.

TELEHEALTH – THE NEW POINT-OF-CARE

Covid-19 accelerated the adoption of digital platforms such as telehealth, and a stat depicts that the increase in telehealth services is made up of almost 70% of all ambulatory visits by mid-April 2020, and prior to the pandemic, that figure was less than 0.01%.[42] Further, the adoption of telehealth channels has seen 75% of providers saying they provide primary care virtually. Approximately 72% of providers use telehealth for chronic care and the other 64% use it for prescription refills.[43]

With 58% of providers being frustrated with the quality of care they provide via telehealth, and 55% of providers experiencing unrealistic expectations from their patients of what can be accomplished virtually,[44] marketers have the ability to ease it with virtual care by enriching their experience and the care of their patients via online mediums.

> It is good to see telehealth formally becoming a real category. While I was a physician, I was doing equal number of physical and telehealth consultations in a day. In the emerging markets where there is a relationship of trust between the physician and the patient, the latter feels free to call their caregivers and even check about minor symptoms or do follow ups, etc. This is now getting formalized in the telehealth category and not just for pre-existing relationships prior to the pandemic, but also for new patients. While this does have its side effects on the physician-patient relationship, the fact can't be denied that it also has great merits in terms of reducing the burden on already loaded healthcare system.

The Covid-19 outbreak brings telehealth to the forefront

Telehealth usage has stabilized with visits being 13-17% higher across all specialties compared to figures prior to Covid-19.[45] As telehealth is now a fixture for healthcare, the digital platforms must provide a seamless experience to HCPs as they meet with patients and have the distribution of messages during virtual visits become a natural extension of educational content for the prescriber to uplift health outcomes.

With the convenience of telehealth, preventive services, prescription refills and routine visits for a chronic illness were being reported as the most common reasons for a visit.[46] Being able to reach physicians while they are providing professional care within telehealth mediums affords marketers the ability to connect with

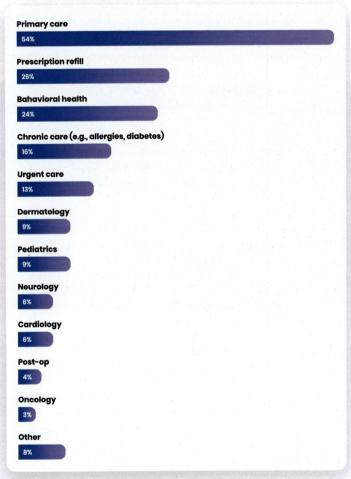

Fig 11: Healthcare services that US telehealth users have accessed via telehealth, by type, Oct 2021

prescribers at decision-making moments as they diagnose and discuss therapy options with their patients. Furthermore, people are turning to telehealth services for a multitude of needs to visit HCPs.

Whether it's seeking to connect with an HCP on the login screen or upon the review of lab results, the precision targeting capabilities offers marketers a virtual forum to reach providers at the digital point-of-care. As the prescribers engage with patients about their health, hyper-targeting communications can enrich the care being provided with educational resources at the fingertips of the clinician.

> Individualize the messages being served to clinicians within telehealth platforms to emphasize messages that will impact the care being provided to the patient.

Leverage data analytics to personalize content directed to prescribers

As interactions are taking place in real-time, the online consultations make it possible for marketers to understand the communication habits of prescribers within telehealth channels to be aware of the stages during an appointment when the messages will have a positive impact on the target audience. The data sets collected on a provider's behaviors on telehealth can progress brands to achieve more impactful campaigns as a clearer landscape into the mindset of the caregiver is generated for organizations.

Primary care visits: **75%**

Chronic car visits: **72%**

Prescription refills: **64%**

Covid-19 screenings: **39%**

Follow-ups after a surgical procedure: **28%**

Fig 12: Ways providers use telehealth platforms

After an initial telehealth visit, the follow-up appointment is conducted virtually approximately 58% of the times by patients.[47]

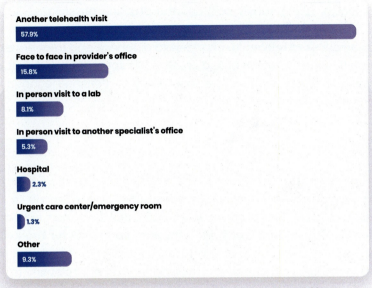

Fig 13: Where did US telehealth users receive their follow-up care after the initial telehealth service?

The attraction of communications within telehealth platforms is the customization that can take place for initiatives to determine the approach that will raise the desired business outcomes. Also, the identification of behavior patterns of HCPs while consulting individuals can embolden exchanges when marketers can decipher when the messages will be most beneficial to share with providers. The metrics gained as more exchanges are delivered in the telehealth setting enable campaigns to be refined to designate the content and timing that's optimal to interact with HCPs to achieve company objectives more efficiently.

According to an AMA Policy Research Perspectives report, the use of video conferencing for patient consults is prominent for dermatology practices (87.3%), urologists (87.2%), pediatricians (82.9%), cardiologists (82%), family and general practice physicians (80.9%) and internists (76.6%).[48] In addition, approximately 83% of psychiatrists used telehealth channels to diagnose and treat patients. Telehealth usage is driven based on an HCP's specialty. Another study disclosed that psychiatrists are most likely to continue conducting telehealth visits moving forward.[49]

The physician's telehealth journey

So, marketers need to establish the segment of providers that are being targeted in the telehealth ecosystem. The nuances in the interactions vary based on an HCP's specialty and their individual preferences regarding telehealth networks are critical for marketers to recognize. For brands to aid clinicians as they hold virtual visits, the digital messages must convey messages that are relevant to the stage of the appointment to assure the exchanges reflect accordingly with their workflow.

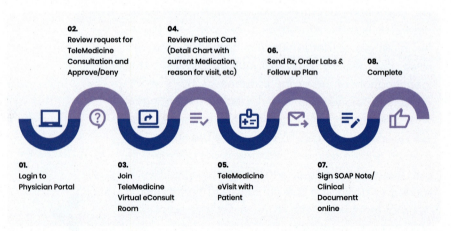

Fig 14: Telehealth workflow of HCPs

Life sciences organizations are challenged to deliver precise communications as an HCP enters the telehealth portal to ensure valuable interactions are held to enrich their experience within the virtual platform. Whether it's a branded message to raise script lift rates or increase awareness about medical developments in the field via unbranded messages, the content must be valuable for prescribers to put the messages to use.

Have messages reach HCPs during opportune moments

Marketers must gather data analytics to identify the right moments to deploy automated communications to prescribers during their telehealth visits. With the use of contextual messages, brands can ensure the exchanges are relevant to the physician's specialty and viewed as an added resource to improve the health outcomes of their patients. By illustrating an understanding of the provider's medical field and previous telehealth habits, precise data-driven content can be shared with HCPs.

Whether it's a banner display or video content that's visible on the physician's screen during their virtual consultation with their patients, the message needs to be relevant to their medical expertise to capture their attention.

Also, the use of technology can be a pain point for HCPs, so sharing enlightening content can minimize apprehensions when a new form of communication appears within a telehealth network. The digital one-on-one sessions taking place remotely don't have to minimize the engagement that physicians experience with their patients. Therefore, marketers supplying additional educational assets can have a superior impact to mimic in-person visits and equip caregivers with vital information to improve their dialogue with patients.

Messages delivered within telehealth networks shouldn't take a caregiver's attention away from their patients.

When brands incorporate actionable insights from data analytics into telehealth visits, a physician's digital setting is supported via seamless communications that are customized to their medical practicing conduct. With the guidance of marketers, clinicians can gain access to additional medical materials that otherwise would have taken dedicated research outside of work hours to obtain and correlate the relation to an individual they met with.

The ability to share hyper-targeted communications assures that the most efficient communications are being served to the target audience within the telehealth portal.

The patient experience must not be diminished

A reported 51% of clinicians felt telehealth would harm their ability to demonstrate empathy with their patients,[50] therefore, the deployment of point-of-care campaigns needs to be designed meticulously to strengthen the HCP-patient relationship. That's an advantage of leveraging messaging platform technologies to employ data analytics to better understand the telehealth workflows to structure communication initiatives efficiently for physicians to drive more personalized interactions with their patients.

In addition, it's essential in all point-of-care messaging campaigns to not take the clinician's attention away from their patient. This is further evidence of the necessity for organizations to interact with caregivers in a manner that empowers them to better communicate with the person they are treating. Empathetic conversations are needed throughout, especially when discussing a patient's ailments, diagnosis, and the advised therapy. Hence, physicians must remain present in the virtual care visit to express compassion while speaking with their patients.

The usage of telehealth platforms in the market isn't expected to diminish with 93% of providers stating in a study that they expect to continue using telehealth once the pandemic ends.[51] Marketers need to invest in programmatic platforms to deliver contextually relevant content to caregivers that are customized based on real-time metrics. With the assurance of the communication materials resonating when it reaches an HCP, brands become top-of-mind as physicians are conversing with their patients to examine their medical circumstances to arrive at a diagnosis.

By having the attention of the HCP, marketers must incorporate telehealth channels into their messaging efforts for them to be a guiding resource during virtual visits. When organizations implement telehealth communications towards prescribers, the data-based analytics must be obtainable to strategically message prescribers during their online session that are tailored to the practicing methods of providers to capture their attention and instill more education pertaining to their specialty.

Jeffrey D. Erb
Entrepreneur and Media Executive, Populus Media

It's important to note that telehealth continues to be on the rise across all therapeutic categories, and that both physicians and patients are viewing it as an integral part of the curriculum of care. As with any new technology, it is important to ensure that both physicians and patients are supported and able to make the most out of this new experience. The ability to leverage HIPAA compliant data provides an unparalleled understanding of the patient and HCP experience, and a means of delivering messaging when it is needed most, in ways that will resonate more effectively with the target audience. Marketing and educational campaigns can be targeted more accurately than ever before and delivered based upon each individual's preferences and unique ways of learning. The message itself can be impacted based upon an analysis of what people's needs are throughout any given consult. It's critical that marketing within the experience doesn't remove the audience from the consult itself, but rather enhances the experience using advanced analytics to provide resources that support the audience based upon where they are in any stage of the journey. The growth of telehealth has empowered every stakeholder within the care process, from physicians and their patients to marketers who support the process and will continue to transform the way care is delivered and managed.

EHR & EHR APPS – COMMUNICATIONS DURING AN HCP's WORKFLOW

EHR systems were initially undervalued during their origination as a database that HCPs utilized to schedule appointments with patients. The proficiency of communicating with physicians as they engaged with their patients led to hesitation from marketers to enter the space for the fear that digital exchanges would distract caregivers during consultations. However, as EHR systems progressed, marketers discovered its ability to be an educational asset to HCPs within the medium by assisting prescribers during patient visits.

Also, as policies are passed to drive the adoption of digital platforms by providers, the advancement of solutions enhances the landscape of EHRs and the usage of the systems by marketers to communicate with clinicians more efficiently.

Exchanges within EHRs have the ability to formulate resources for clinicians in a seamless manner within the online platforms that are part of their workflow. When executed properly, the messages are unified with the channel and reflect the specialty of the caregiver to supply them with an educational resource during patient interactions.

The introduction of policies to advance EHR adoption

The Health Information Technology for Economic and Clinical Health (HITECH) Act was established in 2009 to progress the adoption of health information technology with an emphasis on the meaningful use of EHRs by HCPs. Before this policy was introduced, only 10% of hospitals utilized EHRs.[52] The HITECH Act brought incentives for providers to adopt EHRs and transition away from paper records. By shifting the category towards digital solutions, the efficiency to access patient health records among HCPs via the EHRs intended to improve the management of an individual's medical history. The policy is set to accelerate the use of EHRs beyond a database and for scheduling patient appointments and have the systems deliver meaningful use for the healthcare category.

The Center for Medicare and Medicaid Services (CMS) laid out three stages for providers to adopt and demonstrate meaningful use of EHR technology. These phases began in 2011[53] and are set to define meaningful use as the technology to improve the quality, safety and efficiency of patient care.

Criteria in the Stages of Meaningful Use

Stage 1 Data Capture and Sharing	Stage 2 Advabce Clinical Processes	Stage 3 Improved Outcomes
• Electronically capture health information in a standardized format • Use that information for care coordination processes • Initiate the reporting of clinical quality measures and public health information • Use information to engage patients and their families in their care	• More rigorous for e-prescribing and incorporating lab results • Electronic transmission of patients care summaries across multiple settings • More patient-controlled data	• Improve quality, safety, and efficacy, leading to Improved health outcomes • Decision support for national high priority conditions • Access to comprehensive patient data through patient-centered HIE • Improve population health

Fig 15: *HITECH's proposed five-year timeline*

The objective of HITECH was to achieve interoperability across the EHR ecosystem, so providers could access patient health records across EHR systems regardless of the software being used. As HCPs are tending to their patient, every click of the EHR to input a person's health information into the digital medium took their attention away from their patient. The vision for data interoperability across EHRs would enable physicians to practice medicine instead of documenting past medical events and ailments of an individual.

In 2010, the Affordable Care Act (ACA) continued to progress the use of EHRs in the industry by mandating to advance the way laboratory test results are exchanged and transmitted to EHRs. The policy aimed at positioning the importance of digital tools to progress the industry towards a paperless healthcare system. The ACA elevated the shift for more transparency in EHRs. While physicians were resistant to switch to digital channels, the use of EHRs presented the forum to reform industry practices and instill the use of online solutions to obtain data that will enable clinicians to gain more intel to improve patient care.

The movement for data interoperability in EHR systems

To support the interoperability in the industry, Allscripts, athenahealth, Cerner, CPSI, Greenway, McKesson, and Sunquest founded the CommonWell Health Alliance in 2013. As a not-for-profit trade association, the companies aligned to support individuals and caregivers to have access to health data regardless of where it occurs and to have the data built into health IT at a practical price for HCPs and their patients. This collaboration is meant to achieve base patient health information for continuing care documentation in EHRs and establish interoperability standards in the EHR category.

Then, in 2018, the Centers for Medicare and Medicaid Services (CMS) renamed EHR Incentive Programs to Medicare and Medicaid Promoting Interoperability Programs and shifted the focus to emphasize interoperability, flexibility and patient access to health information.

Further, the passing of the Open, Public, Electronic, and Necessary Government Data (OPEN) Act in 2019 has the vision for non-sensitive, high quality and useful government data to be efficiently managed and accessible to organizations outside of the federal government. In addition, the law requires that the data be machine-readable information to further move companies away from paper documents and advance electronic data record systems. Therefore, this act will further progress data transparency of the digital point-of-care platforms used throughout the industry.

The EHR category evolves digital capabilities

EHR platforms and EHR apps have progressed the way physicians record, organize and access the personal health records of their patients. This online ecosystem continues to evolve the clinician's digital journey to review pertinent information as they tend to their patients. Whether it's an ambulatory or acute EHR system, marketers must navigate the influx of documents that reach providers during their workflow with a data-driven approach that pinpoints the subjects of interest for the caregiver's profession to leverage for messaging campaigns.

Without a singular documentation solution, the health records available to HCPs span a multitude of EHR platforms and EHR apps. As EHR systems are essential to the workflow of clinicians, the usability of the digital mediums lacks efficiency with accessibility to patient health information not always user-friendly. Marketers can share informative messages with providers during their online journey within EHR systems to generate more valuable interactions between prescribers and their patients.

Comprehension of a provider's EHR workflow is integral to distribute messages that align with their medical mindset.

Clinicians spend most of their day connected to EHR networks, which can hamper the quality-of-care patients receive if prescribers are inundated with too many tasks that prohibit their attention towards clinically relevant information. When this occurs, content that can improve patient health outcomes may be missed by the caregiver.

In fact, physicians spend an average of 16 minutes and 14 seconds on EHRs for each patient.[54] During a visit, their attention on chart review (33%), documentation (24%) and ordering (17%) accounted for the majority of the physician's time spent using EHRs.[55] Further, the research points out that specialists spend an average of 16 minutes to enter patient information in an EHR and primary care physicians take 19 minutes,[56] which has resulted in clinicians on an average spending more time documenting the delivery of care instead of providing the necessary care to their patient.

The use of EHRs after clinical hours also persists with prescribers as they respond to messages from their patients, which has further added to the workload of HCPs. The after-hour use of EHRs makes for 11% of the time physicians are on EHRs,[57] and is invaluable for marketers to still capture the attention of HCPs while their focus remains on patients even though consultation isn't taking place.

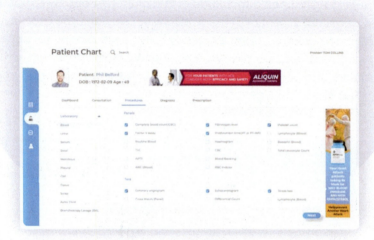

Example of an ad targeting an HCP in an EHR platform

Reaching HCPs on EHR systems

EHR systems are a powerful avenue for brands to communicate with HCPs while the caregivers are mindful of the medical circumstances and therapies that are applicable to their patients. Marketers want to reach their target audience during decision-making moments, and with EHR networks, prescribers are connected to digital platforms which embolden exchanges to take place when it matters the most during an HCP's workflow.

EHR Workflow for HCPs

The digital frontier of EHR systems enables HCPs to have medical records readily accessible for companies to bolster the support for providers to make well-informed assessments of individuals. So, based on the learnings via the content being served to the physician during the workflow, the applicable therapy can be advised to the patient.

Data interoperability should be a priority in healthcare organizations according to 87% of physicians.[58] Nearly the same number of physicians (86%) stated that data interoperability will significantly cut back on the time it takes to diagnose patients.[59] With access to patient data being of use for prescribers, marketers can bolster the efficiency of EHR platforms by sharing relevant messages within their specialty during their workflow.

With this, providers aren't tasked with taking their focus off their patients while having to input additional medical records.

The cultivation of communication strategies within EHR systems must emphasize the necessity of contextual messages being served to the HCP throughout their digital journey. By knowing the landscape of the physician's specialty, messaging efforts can be automated to enrich the way prescribers engage their patients with the latest information that pertains to their condition.

Since 86% of HCPs use EHR systems,[60] marketers have the accessibility to connect with a wide-ranging group of specialists via messages across the digital ecosystem. When organizations have the capability to leverage real-time metrics, then marketers can optimize the content being deployed within EHRs to generate mindfulness for the messages that are distributed based on the prime moments for interactions during a provider's digital journey.

Now 93% of hospitals in the United States have EHR systems, which has risen from 73% just ten years ago.[61] So, communications within EHRs are crucial to ensure the most up-to-date information is accessible for clinicians to gain a comprehensive view of a patient's circumstance to devise an exemplary patient care plan. To progress virtual care, as providers are charting electronically, companies are equipped to comprehend the areas within a physician's specialty to serve clinical content based on the moment of their workflow.

As communications evolve within EHRs, brands are challenged to decipher and understand the HCP's journey to facilitate messages that are non-invasive and advance their proficiency to care for their patients. The use of trigger-based messages provides the precise delivery of meaningful materials that will support the learnings of a physician in his medical field. Based on the prescribing behaviors, marketers can integrate digital exchanges from the login screen for the EHR throughout their online journey to enrich patient interactions.

> Data-driven insights are instrumental to drive effective trigger-based messaging campaigns.

As data flows during an HCP's use of EHRs, data points are amassed by marketers to cultivate a deeper understanding of prescribers to build more high-quality messaging campaigns. The actionable insights then aid marketers in hyper-targeting providers with clinical messages that are based on their prescribing behaviors and communication preferences that will be an enlightening resource during consultations.

While absorbed with patient information as their details are being updated in EHRs, HCPs have a professional mindset and thus have the capacity to be receptive to content that provides an asset to the care of their patient. Therefore, it's important for marketers to measure the moments and types of messages that are most effective to connect with prescribers. When brands can gauge the impact, then it enables marketers to devise campaigns that achieve a higher ROI.

To improve the workflow experience, messages being shared need to reflect the provider's prescribing history and practicing habits to ensure the content is tailored to their professional approach.

Examine when messages resonate with clinicians during their workflow

The data analytics on the messages being served to HCPs affords marketers to discover the areas of value that are being provided to clinicians during their workflow. With the knowledge gained via campaign metrics, marketers can identify the drugs, therapies and additional industry messages that their target audience can connect with. This, in turn, can progress the communication tactics that marketers can implement to secure the desired business outcomes.

The reach at the POC is pivotal for brands to establish a rapport that continues to solidify as the company asserts their clinical communications in an instructive manner that precisely targets HCPs to accommodate their medical needs to better serve their patients.

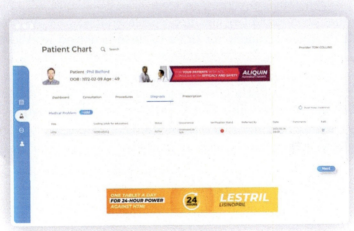

A message served to a clinician during their workflow

Controlling the market share of EHR systems being used

The reach of HCPs via EHR platforms is massive between Epic, Cerner and Greenway Health. Epic leads the category with the largest EHR market share for acute care hospitals at 29%, and records stated that more than 250 million patients have an electronic record in Epic.[62] Meanwhile, Cerner has a 26% stake in the hospital EHR market, which represents nearly 100 million patients.[63]

Epic is the leader in the ambulatory EHR market as well with a 28.21% share of the industry.[64] The controlling portion is lower in this sector for Cerner, which has a 4.32% share and places the company ahead of Greenway Health, which holds 2.91% of the market.[65]

The app stores of Epic App Orchard, Cerner Code and Greenway Marketplace, amass a plethora of digital solutions for clinicians across the online care ecosystem. The technologies covering telehealth, clinical decision support, check-in solutions, workflow efficiency, reporting and analytics, patient care, research, physician documentation and many more, offer tremendous value for the apps to support caregivers throughout their digital workflow.

The virtual environment of the app stores enables EHR systems to present cohesive solutions for HCPs to have a unified workflow. So, providers don't have any apprehension that they are in the wrong channel when presented with a message while utilizing a new EHR app during their online journey. The digital experience enables the environment of EHR apps to be part of a whole package and cultivates an abundance of EHR systems that are accessible to prescribers during their workflow to better support their medical practice.

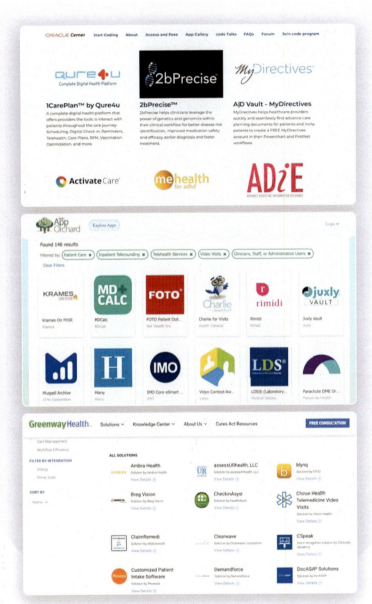

Fig 16: The app stores for Epic App Orchard, Cerner Code and Greenway Marketplace

Whether an HCP is at the diagnostics stage or discussing the treatment options with a patient, the messages on display need to correlate with the digital path the provider takes within an HER. It helps align the content that associates with the stage of their responsibility towards their patient. The messages need to convey real-world evidence during campaigns to illustrate the drugs, treatments and procedures that are beneficial to the health of individuals to support prescribers during decision-making moments.

The digitization of EHR systems needs to be structured to provide clinicians access to patient health records swiftly to minimize their time spent on documenting a patient. It opens more in-depth dialogue to understand their story and appropriately treat the individual. The use of data analytics is instrumental to have a campaign effectively target HCPs to support patient-centered care within EHR systems. As businesses navigate the EHR workflow to share messages that will resonate with physicians, marketers must deliver personalized messages that advance a clinician's medical functions.

At the end of the EHR workflow is the eRx channel, which I will cover in the next chapter, as I detail the optimal messaging strategies to implement within those digital platforms to accomplish more impactful campaigns.

13

eRX TRANSFORMS DIGITAL COMMUNICATIONS

With the massive amount of time HCPs spend using EHR systems, it's natural to include the eRx channel at the end of their digital workflow, so clinicians can write, review, update and communicate a prescription electronically without having to leave an EHR network to join a different platform.

The digital transformation from the Covid-19 pandemic elevated the utilization of eRx platforms with a 72.5% increase in the number of electronic prescriptions written via telehealth during the first month of the outbreak.[66] In 2021, 94% of all medications were e-prescriptions, which was up from 84% in 2020.[67] These digital channels are an optimal path to reach HCPs to boost script lift with 2.12 billion e-prescriptions being filled in 2021, which was an 11% increase from 2020.[68] Also, 2021 experienced approximately 100,000 new prescribers that adopted the online technology to write electronic prescriptions as part of the virtual shift in the category.[69]

When eRx mediums are connected as part of the EHR workflow for providers, marketers are delivered with tailored content that reflects the drugs that would be beneficial to improve the health of the individual. Marketers being able to reach HCPs in a clinical setting embolden messages to be shared to educate their target audience about new drug launches and research studies conducted on medications in the market to improve script lift.

Physicians that use eRx solutions are more efficient in prescribing drugs and communicating the medication to the pharmacy to better support their patients.

Distributing messages on eRx channels

For eRx communications, companies that deploy content to prescribers too early in their workflow can lose traction during campaigns when seeking to raise awareness for a medication that benefits the HCP to be familiar with when tending to their patients. If a message is facilitated too early in a clinician's digital journey, treatment options for their patient aren't top-of-mind for the caregiver and can be forgotten when a treatment is being determined.

However, as the consultation progresses and the circumstance and diagnosis become evident, the informative materials that are shared with providers at the POC garner more consideration.

Marketers have the capabilities to deploy contextual relevant messaging within eRx platforms to deliver effective communications when HCPs arrive at a diagnosis and are advising their patients on their therapy options. By being able to reach clinicians at decision-making moments during their digital workflow, a medication that's the focus of the branded interactions achieves greater recognition from the specialist in the eRx medium.

The use of trigger-based messages that complement the prescribing behavior of the target audience empowers marketers to have a precise understanding of the medications that are prevalent in an HCP's treatment philosophy to comprehend the communications that will be highly valued about new research developments within the category.

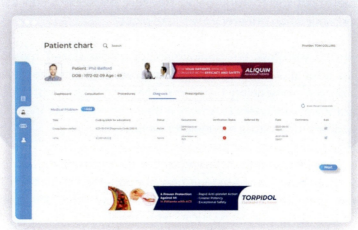

An example of an eRx ad being served to a prescriber

> When marketers are interacting with HCPs on eRx channels, the materials being shared offer immediate therapy options to support their patient's recovery.

Raise awareness when therapies are being considered

Whether marketers deploy a message that's instructive to HCPs to elevate their knowledge about a drug or create awareness about patient assistance offerings for a prescription, organizations can elevate discussions at the prescribing stage of patient visits.

When organizations share educational materials that open the dialogue about the therapy being advised, prescribers can assess whether medication adherence will take place.

In the HCP's workflow, the deployment of trigger-based messages captures educational materials that can resonate with the provider based on their practicing behaviors. The data points obtained on HCPs empower marketers to advance their familiarity with the actions of prescribers to facilitate meaningful exchanges.

With the clinician already knowing about their patient's prescription history, trigger-based messages can support the discussions held between providers and their patients in real-time. The clinical information being served to HCPs strengthens the learnings that physicians have about drug launches and upgrades that are relevant to their specialty to ensure their patients are advised thoroughly on their medication options.

On eRx channels, brands have the digital solutions to effectively promote drugs to their target audience to expand the awareness of the proven impact of the medication that has been achieved during tests and can be shared with their patients. The clinical content being served provides real-world evidence on the impact of medications in their medical field.

For providers, identifying when an individual may benefit from receiving a co-pay card or coupon for a prescription is beneficial to provide the patient assistance to have the person follow the prescribed treatment. During these moments, additional circumstances that may deter a patient from proceeding with the prescribed treatment may come to light.

Measure script life within eRx platforms

It's essential to understand the patient's experience with the prescribed medication and be able to facilitate a more meaningful dialogue about the recommended drugs. When companies can measure the total prescriptions (TRx), new prescriptions (NRx) and new-to-brand prescriptions (NBRx), they can gain comprehensive metrics to decipher the successes and shortcomings of digital interactions.

As the TRx, NRx and NBRx results are being evaluated, data transparency for a company's efforts enriches the knowledge of marketers to determine the affiliation of the content with achieving the business objectives.

When real-time data analytics are available for companies to decipher the performance of communication efforts, marketers are afforded the opportunity to refine messaging tactics within an eRx to optimize content being shared with HCPs. With digital solutions grasping the results garnered from content shared within eRx channels, messaging programs are elevated with the impact being quantified in real-time to maximize the ROI for the campaign.

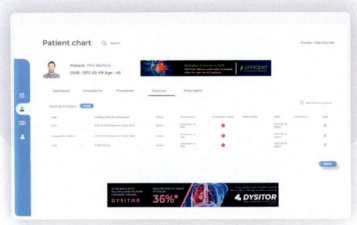

A patient assistance message delivered to a caregiver in an eRx channel

The use of AI provides actionable insights for marketers to formulate campaigns with content that is most effective on eRx channels. By implementing a data-driven approach, marketers are devising messages that have a track record of raising script lift and garnering the attention of the target audience that enables businesses to efficiently streamline communication operations.

 Marketers must embrace AI solutions to analyze messaging campaigns to provide learnings that will guide a superior approach to achieve script lift.

When HCPs are at the end of their workflow on eRx platforms, their mentality is on the patient's health and the treatment that will improve their circumstance. By reaching HCPs while they are prescribing drugs to their patients, the awareness of a provider is heightened when the communications that are taking place can support the health of their patients.

Navigating the workflow is key for marketers to deliver content that will resonate with providers. It's necessary for the messages that are distributed within digital point-of-care platforms to align with the stage that the clinician is at with an individual. For eRx channels, the data analytics that support the hyper-targeted messaging campaigns embolden organizations to elevate script lift with personalized messages based on the HCP's behavior. It will support their determination of the therapy that is suitable for their patients.

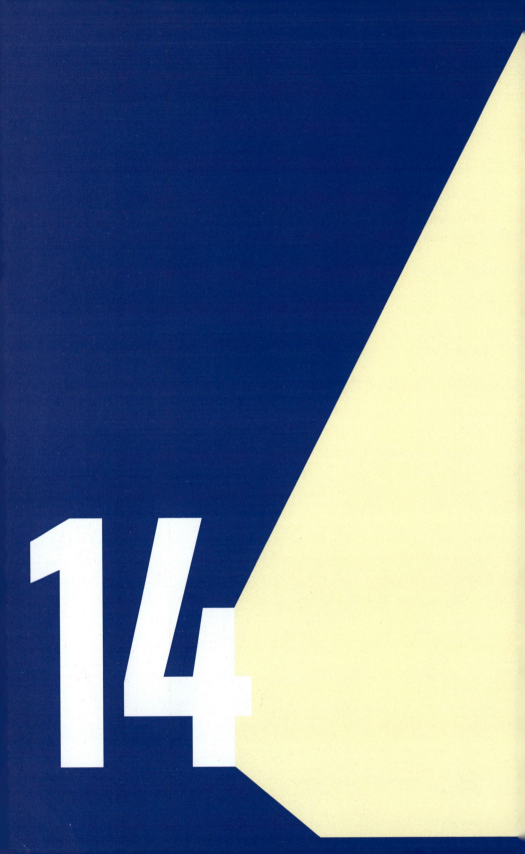

PROVIDING PATIENT ASSISTANCE
DURING POINT-OF-CARE MESSAGING CAMPAIGNS

While I briefly touched upon patient assistance programs during communications within eRx platforms, the value of messages detailing the availability of co-pay cards and coupons provides advantageous interactions with HCPs. When messaging clinicians at the POC, the timeliness of the exchanges can offer invaluable monetary support to patients.

To provide patient assistance, marketers need to deliver communications that prepare physicians to discuss medications while the prescription is being advised to a person. This dialogue inspires conversations that disclose the cost associated with a drug and empowers them to recognize if their patient will adhere to the treatment. These instances can address the monetary barriers of a drug that may be hindering an individual from following their HCP's direction. Prescribers can acknowledge when the financial responsibility of therapy is overwhelming to a person's circumstance and offer an alternative medication.

Being able to learn the rationale of an HCP enriches the proficiency of communications that brands initiate with clinicians to encourage conversations with their patients that may uncover apprehensions when it comes to medication adherence.

> Prescribing the appropriate medication isn't always enough for a patient to recover. HCPs need to be aware of medication adherence to prescribe a drug that is best suited for a patient to overcome their ailment.

The financial barriers to medication adherence

In the United States, a person spends on an average $1,200 per year on prescription drugs.[70] The monetary costs associated with some drugs can be a burden for individuals. So, prescribers need to be aware of all the treatment options that are available, and the patient assistance programs that are available with medications. The recognition of HCPs about the monetary impact associated with drugs in the United States is significant for the clinician to embrace a patient engagement program to communicate therapy options to the individual being treated and align on the treatment that is well suited for the person.

By educating the patient as part of the treatment dialogue, the person will elucidate on the approach they can adhere to, so fewer individuals will drop out of the prescribed care. Also, brands offer financial incentives as part of these programs to motivate patients to stick to the prescribed therapy. In fact, pharma companies spend more than $5 billion on patient support programs per year, but a report revealed that only 3% of patients are using them.[71]

The study further disclosed that lack of awareness is the driving factor with only 23% of patients that participated in the survey stating that they were extremely or very familiar with patient support programs.[72] With 53% of the respondents learning about the programs from their doctors, marketers could enhance the HCP-patient relationship with messages about these offerings that providers can share with their patients during their visits.[73]

If a medication is often more challenging for a patient to afford, it's beneficial for marketers to have the awareness to be able to target a clinician with a similar drug or one that aligns with a patient assistance offering. It would reduce the expense for the person to proceed with the prescribed therapy or seek an alternative option for their treatment.

> Therefore, it's critical for marketers to understand the prescribing behavior of HCPs in the targeted specialty, so provider-patient discussions can take place to prevent their therapy from ending up as part of the 25% of new prescriptions being written that are never filled.[74] This creates a constructive opportunity for marketers to keep providers better informed with messages that aid them as they treat an individual.

Back in 2017, a study disclosed that 69% of patients with at least $250 in annual medication costs were abandoning their medications.[75] As the financial cost of medicines becomes higher for patients, marketers need to recognize those instances to connect with HCPs to facilitate exchanges that lend guidance to overcome financial circumstances. Platform on which clinical decisions are being made is where marketers need to deliver communications to prescribers within their digital channels.

The pandemic has likely grown the number of medications that are being abandoned.

Patients are vulnerable when discussing their medical circumstances and therapies to improve their health, so marketers are wise to serve prescribers with messages during those digital care moments to enrich the dialogue that providers have with their patients to spur on medication adherence. Patients want to make informed decisions, so deploying messages to HCPs enables providers to guide patients toward medication adherence.

When it comes to a person making their health a priority, a report disclosed that 23% of Americans would delay medical treatment or medications they need and another 17% would decline treatment entirely due to affordability issues.[76]

Additionally, for clinicians to know if the prescribed therapy is working, the medication needs to be taken as directed. If prescriptions are going unfilled or used sparingly, it prohibits a clear understanding of the impact the drugs are having on the patient. So, HCPs can expand the financial considerations of a treatment to garner more meaningful exchanges with their patient on the management of their care.

Whether it's a higher-cost drug or generic medication, the prescriber must be confident that their patients will follow the therapy advised. A research indicated that 7% of adults in the US were unable to pay for at least one doctor-prescribed medication for their household the three months prior to the study being conducted in 2021.[77]

The messages that are served to providers can lift the entire burden of determining if the prescriptions will be followed as per the physician's advice. By sharing informative financial content with clinicians, individuals are supported to overcome their monetary difficulties for the betterment of their health. The customization of messages to reflect the treatment history of the provider enables more personalized occasions to bolster the trust between HCP and their patients.

Cultivate communications to drive medication adherence

Meanwhile, around the world patient engagement programs are conducted, but the focus on the initiatives is not driven by finances. Instead, the HCP-patient partnerships are structured by motivating individuals to proceed to adhere to their prescribed therapy. Since inflated drug costs are associated with the United States, brands don't always have to address the monetary challenges in international markets given their prescription drug cost structure. Instead, the focal point of the interactions is to cultivate support sessions that will lead an individual to adhere to the medication.

When money isn't a factor in medication adherence, the patient engagement programs arrange counseling sessions and group meetups to connect like-minded individuals that are going through similar experiences together. By associating with people that have gone through or are in the process of going through a comparable experience, patients have a support system in place to empower them to adhere to their medication. The added guidance instills motivation via personal relationships that encourage individuals to help each other to stick to their therapy and improve their health.

Clinicians are open to receiving real-time messages within EHR systems, but marketers must tailor financial messaging that's relevant to their prescribing behavior to optimize the effectiveness of the communications to providers. Consequently, the messages HCPs receive can empower their long-term care management discussions with their patients.

Only 29% of patients stated in a study that their clinician spoke with them about the cost of a treatment plan.[78] In addition, only one in five patients disclosed that a patient support plan or financial assistance program was covered when a new treatment was presented.[79]

The economical path toward recovery for each patient varies, so marketers must embrace the ability to support individuals by generating awareness about the patient assistance program offerings. Hence, interactions must be conducted with HCPs to raise awareness about financial assistance that exists for a drug being prescribed during their visit.

Marketers must comprehend the digital workflow of HCPs to serve messages to their target audience during decision-making moments such as in eRx channels to ensure all facets of the campaign are precise to enrich the value of messages that are served to providers.

The positioning of patient assistance programs to prescribers

When organizations devise messaging campaigns at the POC, the marketers need to have a commitment to understand the prescribing behaviors of their target audience. The mentality of the prescriber must be captured at the point-of-care to effectively convey messages that represent the circumstances that a provider's patient can face in association with their condition and the therapy being advised.

The usage of point-of-care platforms is essential for brands to serve patient assistance messages to HCPs while treatments are top of mind following the diagnosis being reached during their workflow. As therapies are discussed, organizations are prudent to share monetary materials about drugs that are reflective of the clinician's history to treat an ailment.

By being able to offer guidance during an appointment, marketers can cultivate discussions between providers and their patients that will illustrate if the cost of the medication is an obstacle for the patient that would cause the person to forgo the prescription. Those sensitive conversations can be detected during the consultation and create an opportunity for the prescriber to seek an alternative treatment plan for their patient to still receive a therapy that will improve their health.

Message to raise awareness to a prescriber about the availability of a coupon for a medication

Coupons and co-pay cards provide financial support

Opening communications between prescribers and their patient emboldens the value of the monetary communications that are received from prescribers. If a co-pay card or coupon is shared with the clinician as the prescriber is discussing treatment options, then patient assistance offering may prompt the physician to determine if there are economic constraints that should be considered to treat the person's circumstance.

The use of contextually relevant messages pertaining to patient assistance program provides relevance to clinicians to support their therapy discussions with patients. The distribution of trigger-based messages about a coupon or a co-pay card can provoke the insights necessary for a clinician to determine the financial steps that must be taken to have an individual on a successful treatment plan.

With trigger-based messaging solutions in place, marketers can deliver timely cost-saving alerts to providers within EHR and eRx platforms. These communications about patient assistance offerings being available can be distributed as a text-based, image-based, or as coupon prompt. To improve the awareness around financial savings that providers can instruct their patients about, marketers should observe the data analytics on the types of messages that garner higher script lift for brands and tailor campaigns accordingly.

With personalized communications reflective of an HCP's prescribing behavior, interactions can be enriched to raise health outcomes within point-of-care channels. The ability to reach providers while clinical decisions are being made enables their conversations with their patients to expand therapy discussions to include monetary components of the medication that's being prescribed.

By providing patients with financial savings options when determining their therapy, clinicians can progress a person's health by aligning their fiscal capabilities with the treatment that is suited for their circumstances.

15

TECHNOLOGIES TO ADVANCE
POINT-OF-CARE COMMUNICATIONS

Technological advancements will continue to evolve the point-of-care marketing category as 81% of healthcare executives stated that the pace of digital transformation for their organization is accelerating.[80] Big data is ruling industries and its presence in the life sciences sector is immense for the sophistication of communications within applications and systems across the market. From the progress of artificial intelligence (AI) and machine learning (ML) to the advancements of remote patient monitoring (RPM) and virtual video consultations that 5G will have a role in its utilization throughout the category, the impact will be immense for the modernization of communications to prescribers.

	Remote patient monitoring	% of total	Virtual consultations	% of total	Other	% of total	Total
2020	$0.0	0.0%	$0.16	80.0%	$0.04	20.0%	$0.2
2021	$0.2	33.4%	$0.3	46.6%	$0.1	20.0%	$0.6
2022	$0.5	36.0%	$0.6	44.0%	$0.3	20.0%	$1.4
2023	$1.1	36.3%	$1.3	43.6%	$0.6	20.0%	$3.0
2024	$2.3	37.4%	$2.6	42.5%	$1.2	20.0%	$6.0
2025	$4.6	39.7%	$4.7	40.2%	$2.3	20.0%	$11.6
2026	$9.0	43.1%	$7.7	36.7%	$4.2	20.0%	$20.9
2027	$16.5	47.4%	$11.2	32.3%	$6.9	20.0%	$34.7
2028	$27.4	51.8%	$14.7	27.9%	$10.6	20.0%	$52.8
2029	$40.6	55.3%	$17.8	24.3%	$14.7	20.0%	$73.4
2030	$54.2	57.7%	$20.4	21.7%	$18.8	20.0%	$93.9

Fig 17: Healthcare Cost Savings Worldwide Due to Implementation of 5G, by Use Case, 2020-2030

AI and ML solutions instrumental to customize communications with clinicians

Personalization is an area that a reported 63% of marketing leaders struggle with during campaigns.[81] While 84% of the respondents in a study believe AI and ML technologies enhance the ability of marketers to deliver real-time, personalized experiences, only 17% of those marketers are using it broadly.[82]

By leveraging solutions to capture data sets of HCPs, companies can observe the behaviors of clinicians within point-of-care networks to analyze their actions to detect patterns in their preferences and usage of the communications during their patient care. With the insights delved by AI technologies, the personalization of messaging campaigns is elevated to reflect the prescribed drugs and therapies to patients.

As digital algorithms evolve based on the inflow of data points obtained on HCPs from campaigns that were previously facilitated, marketers will be primed to benefit from the advanced technologies to enhance the programmatic capabilities of brands to reach prescribers. The habits of HCPs in correlation to their intended business outcomes can be monitored to predict the behavior of providers to trigger messages that associate with exchanges that have been successful in past interactions.

> Marketers are going to gain significant learnings from behavior and communication patterns of providers that are detected by AI and ML solutions that will elevate messaging programs.

The use of AI and ML technologies enables marketers to define the initiatives that generate script lift, while it also takes into consideration a reduction in therapies. The awareness of when a physician's behavior delineates from previous actions, the advanced solutions detect the reasons for the diminished script lift rate or additional business outcomes being measured. The collection of data enables intuitive messages to be distributed to target audiences that are customized to their specialty and reflect their prescribing behaviors.

The innovative solutions will cultivate a precise path for life sciences brands by better understanding the clinicians' digital journey to deliver them relevant messages. These data-driven strategies are put in place by measuring the performance of messaging initiatives that have garnered the greatest impact during previous programs.

The combination of AI and ML with human oversight to formulate communication plans provides a powerful resource for marketers to connect with HCPs with well-informed messaging workflows.

Whether the clinician's behavior is happening on a conscious or subconscious level, AI-powered technology provides marketers with intelligence based on data patterns deciphered that will enhance the development and execution of campaigns. Furthermore, the interactions that marketers initiate are customized to the recipient's actions to enrich their experience with the brand.

Transform messaging within an advanced digital ecosystem

According to Allied Market Research, the global healthcare AI market generated $8.23 billion in 2020, and is projected to rise up to $194.4 billion by 2030.[83] AI is growing within the life sciences category and driving the industry demand for personalization during campaigns that demonstrates the company understands the needs of the targeted clinician. So, brands can elevate interactions by incorporating evidence-based medicine research as part of the communications being shared with target audiences to emphasize the scientific evidence in their specialty. They can be used to provide educational assets during their decision-making moments. To optimize patient care, the affiliated research studies in the clinician's field offer an informative resource as caregivers assist their patient.

It's been reported that AI applications are projected to cut annual healthcare costs in the US by $150 billion in 2026,[84] with an outlook for the healthcare model to shift from disease treatment to health management.

The role of data-generating devices

The pairing of AI with data-generating devices such as wearables, digital therapeutics and EHR apps, empowers marketers to better understand HCP's practices in their medical field. The behavior patterns detected among the collected and examined data lead to improved campaigns with better performance metrics based on the learnings gained via AI solutions. In addition, the actionable insights detected and analyzed by AI position brands to be notified of trends taking place within their category to refine and optimize communications to providers.

As the optimal use of AI-powered messaging technologies progress in the virtual point-of-care space, the workflow of target audiences is discovered to afford marketers greater intel on when to share messages with their target audience. The next best action for communications to providers can be executed under the guidance of the findings uncovered by an AI solution.

With the utilization of wearables and digital therapeutic devices, providers have the ability to improve the virtual care experience of patients. Whether via an Apple Watch, connected thermometers and stethoscopes or glucometers, caregivers need to be able to monitor their patients remotely when an individual seeks a virtual visit with their physician.

Now, with this level of intel accessible to providers, marketers need to be able to facilitate communications that are seamless with the interactions being conducted via telehealth channels. The online spectrum will expand the data analytics available on the behaviors of HCPs with the convenience of virtual visits with clinicians.

The AI analysis of data points will elevate the predictive capabilities for marketers to better comprehend the digital journey of providers to enhance their experience with messages that are reflective of how they are utilizing the respective digital platform with patients for the facilitation of precise messages. The data-based insights from AI will better position physicians towards providing preventive care, which presents the opportunity for marketers to have their exchanges reflect those communication methods that will enable brands to identify the type of educational messages that will be beneficial and timely for HCPs.

Connected devices will elevate patient care

With 320 million consumer health and wellness wearables expected to be shipped this year, and that figure expected to rise up to 440 million by 2024,[85] the incorporation of the mobile devices emphasizes the frontier for data that prescribers will have on their patients. As connected devices bring providers closer to their patients virtually to monitor their health and diagnose and treat their health ailments, companies must ponder over those additional learnings to better tailor messages to providers.

The elevated monitoring ability provides additional data sets of the HCP-patient relationship that can be enhanced with precise messages that are shared with prescribers during their digital journey. With clinicians having the capacity to monitor patients throughout the life cycle of medication via connected devices, marketers can comprehend the practices and behaviors of providers more thoroughly to distinguish the impact of messages being served throughout their virtual workflow.

With real-world data being accessible on the therapy path of patients, the elevated guidance for interactions with providers dictates the route to the prescriber with educational materials that reflect their interests in their medical field. The collective data analytics will be a remarkable asset for marketers to progress communications in the evolving landscape of messages within point-of-care networks.

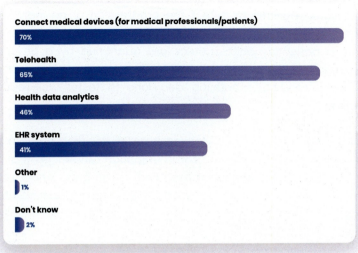

Fig 18: Healthcare Technologies with Biggest Impact in the Next Five Years According to UK/US Healthcare Professionals*, May 2021

Correlating data points to the prescribed treatments

With various data streams collecting metrics on the performance of communications across the online channels, the progression of interactions can be measured efficiently to refine strategies that will grow as virtual habits of prescribers expand within the point-of-care ecosystem. The volume of data that is obtainable in the category opens the opportunity for relevant communications to be facilitated to prescribers for assisting them with informative messaging programs. As the monitoring capabilities of wearables and therapeutic devices expand, these technologies will further bolster the context of a patient's medical circumstance to enable clinicians to make more informed decisions when determining the treatment plan for their patient.

The evolution of wearables will advance the care provided to individuals as virtual consultations are held with the insights gathered via connected devices to detect the progression of an individual's treatment and abnormalities that may signal the need for additional care. As a patient's health metrics are quantified by a physician, organizations have an advantageous opportunity to use the learnings of an HCP's medical practicing decisions to foster well-rounded interactions.

By embracing data analytics derived from AI-powered platforms, AI and ML algorithms can identify communication tendencies that can be leveraged to optimize messaging strategies and further personalize interactions with clinicians to garner a higher ROI for a business.

> Advanced AI and ML technologies will lessen the challenges that organizations face to effectively reach clinicians within point-of-care networks. As the solutions are embraced, the digital capacities of marketers will continue to accelerate in the sector, as the latest messaging capabilities offer a more efficient way to personalize interactions with HCPs. The intelligence implemented in messaging platforms will lead brands to better target audiences, measure outcomes and facilitate messages to embolden prescribers to provide better patient care.

16

IDENTIFYING THE RIGHT APPROACH FOR A MESSAGING CAMPAIGN

There isn't a one-size-fits-all approach to point-of-care communications. So, companies need to identify the platforms that are most suitable to execute messaging initiatives to achieve the sought-after business outcomes. Across POC networks, organizations need to align campaigns with the type of channels that will embolden their message to reach HCPs at the optimal moment. Even when the content is crafted perfectly, the communication can miss the mark if it's delivered when the target audience isn't receptive to a message.

Brands can empower caregivers during decision-making moments with personalized exchanges to improve patient care. In addition, the way the communications are served to HCPs needs to be seamless. When a message appears within an EHR system, the target audience should be viewing the communication as part of their online experience within that platform. The medium selected for a campaign needs to have the messaging formats integrated within their system to have the messages distributed as part of the design of the digital network.

Consequently, data analytics are pivotal for companies to determine the type of health information technology (HIT) platform that would be suitable for their brand's campaign. The access to metrics emboldens marketers to make data-based decisions to optimize their communication plans to HCPs.

Data points signify the superior moments for interactions

As I've covered, the data sets accessible to marketers permit companies to strengthen their comprehension of the workflow of their target audience. The data across eRx, telehealth and EHR networks illustrates the usage habits of providers and the moments during their workflow when they are most receptive to messages from brands.

The data points on the digital journey of prescribers highlight the communications landscape across the point-of-care ecosystem for marketers to devise messaging plans. The ability to pinpoint the moments within an online channel that will be suitable for a clinician enables companies to optimize their budget.

The use of programmatic technologies further advances the messaging proficiency of brands to make data-driven decisions for the way campaigns are executed. The accuracy of programmatically derived campaigns ensures the messaging being displayed to the clinician is relevant to their medical field.

When the campaign is in development, the target audience needs to be identified by their NPI number, specialty, location or additional demographics that pertain to the sought-after HCPs.

> The collection of data on the target audience positions marketers to better customize messaging campaigns that HCPs find beneficial.

Preparing to deploy a messaging campaign

While marketers are narrowing down the way to reach their target audience, they must factor in the type of messages they want to distribute within a point-of-care channel - will it be a video or a display piece of content that will be served to HCPs?

Further, organizations have to factor in the moments during a clinician's journey that will achieve desired results for the company. Whether the message is going to be branded or unbranded is another critical piece for the development of communication initiatives to consider before the campaign goes live. Also, marketers must decipher the terms that will determine the success of the campaign. Is it generating awareness, script lift or the use of a coupon? Before executing a digital exchange, an organization needs to align with the platform that enables them to reach their target audience when they are most receptive to the company's message.

When seeking to implement a programmatic project, it's imperative to align with a technology partner that offers the resources to optimize communication to maximize the ROI of the campaign. With a partner that provides data analytics that are supportive to enhance interactions, business outcomes achieved via the collaboration will be elevated. With a comprehensive overview of point-of-care campaigns, a brand can unite with the ideal HIT platform that understands the messages being facilitated in the campaign and the manner that's essential for their audience to embrace the communications from a brand.

As I covered the messaging capabilities of telehealth, eRx and EHR systems, each type of medium has its benefits for an organization to reach HCPs at the POC. The online platforms are mighty digital resources to deliver messages to providers that will lead companies to raise their business outcomes. While marketers will utilize various combinations of virtual systems to interact with clinicians, the expanding networks within the category enable marketers to balance communications across the digital point-of-care channels.

Develop a plan for point-of-care communications

When devising a communications program, the company's business objectives must be identified, so marketers can formulate the plan that will enhance the organization to achieve the corporation's goals.

Regardless of the online platform, marketers should keep the exchanges to HCPs concise, so that the provider is not distracted from their patient. Further, the interactions need to be received as a resource for the prescriber. Thus, the content should be positioned in a manner that doesn't challenge therapy behaviors and decisions of the caregiver.

Identify the messaging formats that are beneficial to the campaign

Whether it's a text, banner or video format for a message, an organization shouldn't direct their entire campaign in a single structure. Companies need to embrace data analytics to examine the results of campaigns, so messaging tactics can be refined for current and future initiatives. When brands are in the early stages of utilizing point-of-care platforms as part of their messaging repertoire, then being able to measure the performance of messages in real-time is of tremendous value to maximize the results of a campaign.

By gaining actionable insights in real-time, the budget for a brand is optimized with metrics being assessed to ensure the communications are going down well with the target audience within the online channel. Further, organizations can identify the platforms that are garnering a higher ROI for the business to efficiently allocate funds for digital interaction endeavors.

By comprehending the workflow of HCPs, marketers can formulate the messages that will drive traction to achieve the company's ambitions. As with any new communication undertaking, a brand should experiment with communication strategies for point-of-care platforms to learn the approach that is most beneficial to an organization.

HOW DOES POINT-OF-CARE MESSAGING HELP

For platforms to optimize the value of offering messaging campaigns within their HIT sites, the design to allocate messages must support HCPs while tending to patients at the POC. The challenge that platforms in the life sciences category face is that brands don't know the appropriate moments to share messaging with providers to enhance the clinician's experience within point-of-care channels.

Design a platform that seamlessly integrates messaging campaigns

The digital environment for prescribers needs to be strengthened to warrant the distribution of online exchanges within point-of-care platforms to caregivers. With the use of virtual care mediums, platforms have the ability to serve informative messages to physicians. However, what approach and considerations must a platform factor in when implementing communication means within their point-of-care network?

Is an HCP going to view interactions with brands as beneficial? Are the communications going to be branded or unbranded? At what portions and dimensions within the medium will a message be shared? Which components of supplying campaigns does a platform need to examine and formulate a plan around while not alienating the HCPs using their platform?

The online forum for interactions is evolving, so it's a necessity for platforms to navigate the optimal ad formats, frequency and content that can bolster the efficiency of campaigns during the early stages of adopting programmatic solutions to enhance offerings to reach HCPs during their digital journey.

> With data analytics comprehending the HCP experience on their sites, platforms can optimize their ad slots to ensure the deployed campaigns benefit the prescriber's experience. Further, sell-side companies can decipher the high and low-impact areas of messaging efforts during a provider's workflow to improve the offerings of their HIT platform.

The hesitation of platforms to introduce ad slots

From online channel disruption of the HCP's experience to data privacy, supply-side organizations may have apprehensions to be involved with point-of-care messaging programs. So, I'll delve deeper into the platform's perspective on digital point-of-care communication plans. Sell-side platforms face challenge in successfully integrating content within a HIT platform, but when executed wisely with the clinician's experience remaining the focal point of the platform, a point-of-care network can effectively distribute messages to HCPs. Prescribers are receptive to messages at the POC with a study having disclosed that 87% of HCPs want either all virtual or a mix of virtual and in-person meetings even after the pandemic ends.[86]

So, communications must not disturb their interactions with their patients. When platforms can formulate an approach to elevate the provider's digital journey within a point-of-care network, then it's advantageous for the caregivers to become more well-informed in their specialty.

With the analysis of the results of campaigns to identify the traction that was achieved with prescribers, platforms can identify the type of interactions that are of most significance to providers. The metrics on the ad slots showcase the type of formats, timing and content that enhance the prescriber's experience with the platform. The data analytics amassed enable platforms to ensure an optimized design is implemented to disseminate content.

A supply-side platform empowers organizations with a comprehensive understanding of the way prescribers utilize the platform as part of their workflow to have sell-side offerings that enrich the high-value touchpoints with HCPs. Consequently, this leads platforms to embolden the online communications to clinicians by opening up opportunities to serve trigger-based messages during the provider's digital journey.

Operate campaigns to enrich the digital environment

By being able to guide marketers within their platform to cultivate communication opportunities with HCPs, platforms can uplift the value of their HIT platform by supplying informative messages that resonate with the targeted physician.

The standard for high-value messages helps platforms to yield higher returns for facilitating meaningful campaigns for marketers that raise their business outcomes. As the caregiver intakes information while engaging with their patients, it provides them the ability to spur conversations about treatments and drugs that can be beneficial to the health of a patient. The continuation of education is essential in the medical field, so when HIT platforms create a learning environment for clinicians, the medium is highly regarded beneficial for the sector.

> It's essential for platforms to formulate a design to provide cohesion within the digital channel by blending the messages from marketers in a seamless manner that doesn't intrude upon the HCP's usage of the system.

Meanwhile, companies need to be aware of the messaging capabilities that observe data privacy regulations, which is a necessity for platforms to offer an environment for communications to be shared in a compliant manner. In addition, the intel gained by sell-side companies about the usage of campaigns empowers automated initiatives in the point-of-care category to modernize messaging efforts based on data analytics.

Platforms can support medication adherence

With the messages being ushered into their virtual experience, prescribers can obtain the knowledge to progress meaningful dialogue with their patients about their health circumstances and adherence toward the prescribed therapy. As patients trust their physician has the medical insights to treat their ailments, platforms must conceive the way digital exchanges can appear at the POC to resonate with prescribers, so the caregiver is more knowledgeable about therapies pertaining to their patient.

With HIT sites, platforms can offer messaging formats that can provide information to HCPs. A critical part of patient care is medication adherence, but when the messages to be served to providers are known, then organizations on the sell-side can enhance the provider-patient interaction that can take place with the latest medical developments being shared during patient visits. It will help better educate patients about their therapy to adhere to the prescribed medication.

As caregivers use point-of-care channels, the communication offerings of supply-side businesses enrich the treatment discussions that can develop between HCPs and their patients. Whether it's a message about a specific drug or a coupon, the more potential apprehensions towards a therapy that are uncovered during the visit empowers prescribers to lead patients to improve their health. The deployment and format for when exchanges are received by providers enhance consultations during decision-making moments of a provider's journey.

When HIT platforms provide additional resources via timely and educational messages, the usefulness of the medium rises with marketers. The representation of the importance of setting forth providers on the path to achieving optimal health outcomes for their patients showcases the sentiment a platform wants to impart to clinicians operating on their site.

When a platform can present a communication ecosystem that illustrates the consideration for the workflow of HCPs, better results follow for patients because of the extensive design that considered all facets of the way messages are received by clinicians during their workflow.

As prescribers navigate digital channels, the platforms that seamlessly integrate informative communication offerings to support the HCP experience on point-of-care platforms will cultivate the trust of clinicians to utilize the digital channel as part of their digital journey to treat patients.

18

AN ASSESSMENT OF THE POINT-OF-CARE MESSAGING LANDSCAPE

As virtual care is embraced by HCPs and patients, the communications that take place within the digital channels have an impact on the relationship cultivated during visits. With a reported 51% of clinicians believing that telehealth will negatively impact their ability to demonstrate empathy with their patients,[87] the interactions offered from platforms can empower caregivers to not lose trust of their patients in an online setting.

Digital transformation will become moderately or very important during the next three years, according to providers in a 2021 survey.[88] Thus, as the landscape of point-of-care channels progresses, the requirements of clinicians using the virtual networks must be aligned with the desired experience of HCPs.

The ad formats must be devised to be helpful to physicians and marketers must understand the way a prescriber practices within the digital channel to improve the offerings that better equip them to care for their patients. However, it's up to the platforms to determine if the introduction of messages within the HIT site is suitable to proceed with to achieve the company's business objectives.

Strategically plan communication offerings

Messages being shared with HCPs should enrich the experience of the clinician and not disrupt their virtual channel environment. The focal point of communications for sell-side companies is the HCP's experience. If the digital atmosphere that's created within an online system doesn't resemble the expectations of the HCP, the user will opt for another platform that more seamlessly enriches their digital journey.

A report discovered that 62% of HCPs are "overwhelmed" by product-related promotional content they receive from drugmakers.[89] So platforms must ensure the channel isn't oversaturated with messages directed at clinicians. Meanwhile, 70% of HCPs stated in a survey that pharma reps "do not completely understand their needs and expectations."[90] Hence, it's necessary for the interactions held by HIT platforms to demonstrate an appreciation for the clinician's workflow to achieve an improved line of communication to them.

> Formulate ad slots that are meaningfully placed within the HIT platform that will enrich the HCP's digital environment.

Platforms need to have point-of-care platforms be supportive of prescribers during patient visits to ensure their benefits are substantial to use the channel while HCPs are caring for their patients. Also, supply-side organizations don't want to deter providers from using their system because the messages are being perceived as coercive and are viewed as a distraction.

Communications across the point-of-care landscape are essential to reach caregivers without taking their attention away from their patients. The exchanges held via HIT platforms must be facilitated in a manner that creates a relationship which enables HCPs to have an ongoing dialogue with brands, making a clinician diagnose and prescribe therapies more efficiently.

The structure of point-of-care communication offerings

As with any new offerings within a platform, there is hesitation as to how it will be received by the target audience. Thus, it's pivotal for the messages being displayed within the platform to be incorporated into the platform effortlessly.

When ad formats don't align with the digital setting of a channel, it's disastrous and the user experience will suffer. The communication offerings that are featured need to be an extension of the channels, so the cohesion for the medium is consistent throughout the system.

When operating point-of-care networks, messaging offerings shouldn't overtake the ability of providers to access and document a patient's medical health records.

As the communication landscape evolves, platforms need to decipher the structure that's advantageous to distribute content to their prescribers. By being able to assess the usage of ad slots with data analytics, statistics can guide a decision that if an ad offering is feasible within the channel or not. In addition, the data compiled can illustrate the placements that are most valuable for clinicians to receive messages from marketers.

The high-performing ad slots can elevate the educational content that can be shared with providers to advance their knowledge in their medical field. A reported 43% of providers stated that improving care quality continues to be a key priority.[91] As marketers reflect on the communication methods that resonate with HCPs, the evolution of messaging at the POC will progress to transform interactions across the digital ecosystem.

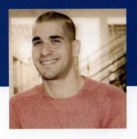

Angelo Campano
Sr. Vice President, Market Engagement at OptimizeRx

Point-of-care messaging to drive 'connected health' is personalizing healthcare for patients, marketers, and healthcare professionals (HCPs). Companies are investing heavily in this sector because they recognize connected health's power and untapped potential. This emerging field encompasses countless connected digital channels — specialized care delivery platforms, mobile, electronic health records and plug-ins, and telehealth. These mediums point to a theoretical model for health management, where devices, services, and interventions are designed specifically to address the patient's needs.

 Health-related data can be shared so the patient can receive care proactively and efficiently. Marketers should aim to have their connected health tools provide a similar experience. As HCPs and patients continue to interact with the healthcare system through connected digital channels, we expect to see tools that incorporate patients' histories and create customized regimens that examine patients' risk profiles and accordingly suggest them lifestyle activities. The combination of personalized tools can help marketers make more informed decisions about wellness communications delivered to HCPs and their patients. Combining data sources could produce a holistic digital view of the patient and will help HCPs intervene at the right moment. Connected health is beneficial because it connects the dots in the patient's healthcare journey. The term has recently gained traction, with marketers, physicians, and technology professionals touting how these tools can efficiently revolutionize healthcare.

19

THE DECISION TO INTRODUCE AD SLOTS
WITHIN A POINT-OF-CARE PLATFORM

Personalized communication is the key for platforms to enrich the HCP experience within a virtual channel. However, to facilitate point-of-care campaigns for providers, it is important that the experience of clinicians is taken into consideration to succeed in enhancing the digital environment.

Online point-of-care networks are at the fingertips of caregivers, so HIT platforms can present communication moments between life sciences brands and HCPs within digital systems that serve educational exchanges throughout their workflow. When the physician gains a positive experience from a company's ad, then the knowledge can be passed along to their patient.

In addition, the ad slots that are offered to life sciences brands need to be analyzed to determine the manner that will be beneficial to display informative content to HCPs without disrupting their virtual journey.

Introducing ad slots

The creation of ad slots brings a monetary component for a platform to expand their business revenue. However, the introduction needs to be facilitated with the mindset that the communications enrich the learnings that clinicians receive within their medical field that improve the care that's provided to their patients.

When caregivers are able to identify that the messages being shared relate to their specialty, then the person can recognize the usefulness of the communications being received to improve their knowledge in their sector.

Platforms need to demonstrate a superior experience via the customized messages that are shared within the site, so any apprehension from the HCP subsides as the exchanges are perceived as supportive for the provider's profession. The individualized interactions enable platforms to facilitate campaigns when the communications are optimal for clinicians. By having messages shared at optimal moments with prescribers, caregivers can strengthen their confidence in their medical expertise.

Once HCPs recognize the value of messages from life sciences brands, they are open to the communications taking place within point-of-care platforms.

While cultivating the trust of HCPs by providing informative resources to them as they are utilizing the platform, that level of transparency must proceed when collecting data on individuals. As providers are benefiting from the customized interactions, it's imperative for data transparency to continue with the prescribers using the POC network, and communicating the way their data points are being used.

Data collection practices

Platforms can garner faith in HCPs to opt-in to share their information by detailing the use of the data being collected. Therefore, it helps to be upfront about the benefits that are achieved with tailored communications from the amassed first-party data that was gained via their behaviors within the platform.

With a comprehensive understanding of the physician's use of the channel, platforms can pinpoint the interactions within the medium that can elevate the offerings to marketers. The data points equip platforms to develop more impactful communication offerings to aid organizations in the space to deliver more precise digital exchanges to clinicians.

Further, the ability to obtain data analytics that reflects the success of ad slots to reach HCPs illustrates the impact garnered via a seamless setting to connect marketers with providers at the point-of-care. HCPs are focus of point-of-care campaigns, so platforms need to reassure clinicians that their patient's information isn't accessible to be used as part of the messaging methods.

Test ad slots to arrive at the optimal placements

As platforms ponder a rollout of ad slots in their platform, it's best to proceed with a trial period before implementing the communication offering throughout the medium. This enables a platform to see the impact of the placements of messages. As the offering is tested, platforms can identify any potential areas that cause a negative experience which needs to be addressed, while also being able to note the high-performing messaging placements within the channel.

The experimental period enables platforms to gain data analytics to examine the impact of messages being displayed and examine if the ad placements within the site impacted the user experience and the reputation of the company. The metrics also provide greater insights into the placements and types of communications that achieved more meaningful interactions with providers.

Supply-side companies have to be mindful of the user experience and embrace the data findings that reveal any changes in how prescribers are using the platform as a result of a message being displayed. With those learnings, the moments when messages are displayed and the formats that are used can be adjusted to refine the implementation of campaigns with the point-of-care network.

When the ads are rolled out in smaller increments, HCPs aren't taken aback when using the channel. With a thorough understanding of how clinicians use the point-of-care system, platforms can navigate the alignment of ads within the point-of-care site that continues to provide a smooth experience to physicians during their workflow.

20

MESSAGING FORMATS TO FACILITATE
POINT-OF-CARE CAMPAIGNS TO HCPs

When preparing to distribute messages within POC platforms, the dimensions for the ads need to blend into the channel in a cohesive manner. The format for ads must match the digital environment that's established within the medium. When the messages merge for a unified integration within the digital ecosystem, then a platform combines the distribution of the campaign that will proceed naturally within the point-of-care spectrum.

Select the appropriate ad formats

Therefore, platforms must decipher the dimensions that will be beneficial to utilize with the point-of-care system. Whether it's a leaderboard, banner, skyscraper, square or another dimension, the design of the digital medium will garner a favorable user environment for HCPs. The selection of dimensions that are offered with a HIT platform offers guidance on how the messages are positioned to clinicians.

Fig 19: Provide the optimal performance by selecting the optimal ad slot dimensions

Platforms have to identify the messages that are suitable for the point-of-care network to ensure the appearance doesn't disrupt the workflow of providers. The determination of the ad slots that are featured within a point-of-care platform helps platforms to make marketers get familiar with the formats that are achievable for a campaign.

Platforms must be mindful of the appearance of messaging campaigns being conducted via their site to ensure that their partners have the necessary communication options to choose from to display their communications in the optimal manner. Thus, the more variety that can be presented in a seamless manner, the greater the appeal is for marketers to align with the platform to disseminate the messages to prescribers. Also, platforms must ensure the dimensions of the ad slots don't hinder the creativity of marketers to craft exchanges to reach HCPs.

> The ability to offer a multitude of formats enriches the appeal of the channel to marketers and provides flexibility for a campaign to be executed with the platform as the company envisioned.

Identify the value of ad slots

Now, once the formats have been integrated within the site, it's essential for platforms to obtain data analytics for the traction that is gained via the placements across the channel. By doing so, platforms can learn the success and shortcoming of its ad dimensions and identify offerings that need to be refined to optimize selling particular ad slots.

With the metrics attained, the platforms can learn the performance of ad slots to signify the value presented to marketers and enrich the support towards implementation of messaging campaigns. Platforms are able to optimize the performance of communications with data obtained, depicting the effectiveness of the ads placed within an allotted segment of the medium. Therefore, the metrics of the dimensions empower platforms to better advise their partners on an ideal approach to deploy communications in the channel.

Timing is crucial for communications at the POC. So as clinicians are navigating their workflow, platforms can monitor and examine the ad slots that lead to more impact at the various stages of virtual care. When platforms identify the allotted placements for ads within their point-of-care system, the hyper-relevant information can be facilitated efficiently to elevate the expertise an HCP can attain in their specialty at opportune moments.

21

ADVANCE THE DEPLOYMENT OF TELEHEALTH OFFERINGS

The telehealth sector is projected to reach $20 billion in revenue in the United States by 2027.[92] Throughout the duration of a patient's virtual care visit, platforms can enrich the digital environment on an HCP's screen. With 93% of providers stating in a study of their plan to continue to use telehealth platforms after the Covid-19 pandemic,[93] the online experience has to progress to elevate the care that is provided to patients. So, platforms in the category must bolster the development of messaging offerings to enhance the benefits of telehealth platforms to assist prescribers while treating their patients.

Providers have shared that primary care (75%), chronic care (72%) and prescription refills (64%) were the most popular types of care that were delivered via telehealth networks.[94] Consequently, platforms have to shape the landscape of communication capabilities to complement the manner the ecosystem is being utilized. By doing so, platforms can establish communication offerings that exhibit the most value to marketers.

Establish ad formats that support marketers increase business outcomes

With script lift as a sought-after metric in the life sciences industry, the interactions facilitated in real-time generate interest for companies to align with platforms for messaging campaigns that have a track record to raise business outcomes. The formation of ad slots strategically placed throughout online consultations unlocks dynamic campaigns that can be amplified with integration into a telehealth platform to deliver real-time messages.

Accordingly, the recognition of the performance of ad slots during the digital interaction is significant for platforms to invent meaningful offerings that demonstrate the impact of communications deployed within a telehealth network. The ability to design an online atmosphere based on data analytics allows platforms to refine a messaging campaign that can be run on the platform without jeopardizing the physician's environment.

By being able to address the pain points of caregivers, the timeliness of a message is tactfully displayed within telehealth networks to deliver an added resource for prescribers in a manner that reflects the stages of a virtual care visit. platforms can bring quality messages to the forefront with the design of the dimensions for ad slots that provide continuity throughout the digital setting.

Fig 20: Video visits make up 88% of telehealth visits

With **video visits being held 88% of the time in telehealth systems**,[95] supply-side companies have to establish the foundation for visual ads to amplify real-time communications that are held within the channel.

Establish ad slots that drive quality interactions

Also, during telehealth visits, the clinician's attention must remain on the patients. Therefore, the positioning of ad formats within the medium must enhance the quality of the consultation that a patient receives.

> Platforms that provide the ability to effectively reach specialists in their medical field are highly regarded in the market.

The foundation of communication offerings needs to be supported to embolden conversations held with patients. So, the structure of messaging slots needs to be devoted to strengthening the HCP-patient relationship and not diminishing the communications that take place within telehealth channels.

Thus, the ability to tailor messages to connect with providers during their workflow is instrumental for deploying communications. It's a necessity for the virtual exchanges supplied to marketers to integrate effortlessly into programs.

Platforms are challenged to mimic an in-person office visit, so communication offerings should replicate the phases of consultation when the conveyed messages are beneficial to caregivers. The framework for communications cultivates the facilitation of content that aligns with the moments taking place as the HCP converses with their patient.

A message is distributed to a clinician using a telehealth network

The arrangement of ad slots within telehealth networks enables platforms to identify the moments during interactions when messages will be welcomed and would garner the greatest connections for marketers.

When the ad slots within the platform unify the experience, then the usefulness is elevated by the platform for materializing the opportunities to reach physicians in an effortless manner.

Telehealth has transformed the practices of clinicians in the space. Now, providers expect any messages to be connected to their digital journey and interactions must not interrupt their workflow. For platforms to support prescribers to provide comprehensive care, telehealth mediums need to share messages that help guide their visit with patients to improve the online patient care setting.

22

EHR & EHR APPS FOSTER NEW MESSAGING
OFFERINGS DURING AN HCP's JOURNEY

The seamless nature of EHR platforms and EHR apps is invaluable when crafting the structure of platforms to distribute messages during the virtual workflow of HCPs. The digital EHR ecosystem has been built to improve the online professional setting for providers to better tend to their patients.

While a platform may view the addition of ad slots as clutter on the screen to prescribers, the communications from companies being distributed isn't a drawback to the user's experience when the construction of the messaging offerings is developed to offer exceptional aid to caregivers within the channel.

Devise communication formats for a positive platform experience

The contemplation of a negative impact on the HCP's workflow is natural for platforms. Therefore, the mindset must be set on identifying the elements within EHR platforms and apps that don't intrude on the provider's work, while opening a line of communications that can support the medical professionals using the EHR system.

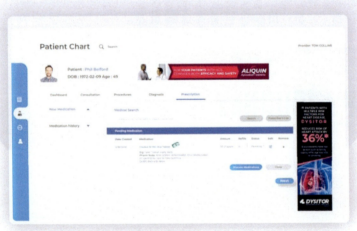

An example EHR ad being viewed by a physician

The use of metrics to gauge the channel experience guides platforms on the rollout of the type of ad slots that enrich the digital journey of clinicians. By being able to monitor and analyze the segments within the EHR system that garner traction for their partners, platforms can establish suitable communication offerings that don't take an HCPs attention away from their patient within the digital medium.

Further, the use of AI solutions to examine data analytics is a valuable resource for supply-side companies to refine messaging formats within the system. Also, data-driven learnings identify the high-impact moments to provide communication opportunities during a clinician's workflow to continue to learn the behavior patterns within the channel to optimize the positioning of ads within the EHR system. By obtaining the data sets, platforms are able to formulate an online setting to offer marketers the ability to embolden interactions with HCPs within an EHR network.

Physicians devote 62% of their time per patient review on EHRs.[96] So, platforms can decipher when their operations can facilitate clinical alerts that can effectively distribute messages to support digital interactions. In addition, savvy platforms understand the benefits of the performance of ad slots to optimize exchanges with providers that will maximize their financial arrangements with partners to run their communication initiatives.

Select digital solutions that amplify messages for marketers

The communication tools available from platforms inspire more meaningful relationships for brands and patients to flourish in the evolving landscape. With EHR platforms, they can devise the communication offerings to virtually be by the side of providers as they engage with their patients. Thus, formulating trigger-based messaging opportunities for marketers emboldens platforms to emphasize the real-time interactions that can be facilitated within the EHR medium.

By doing so, platforms can provide a solution for marketers to overcome the barriers of reaching clinicians with messages that resonate with them because the message is being distributed to reflect the precise time during the HCP's journey when the communication is most helpful.

The facilitation of messaging campaigns at optimal moments during a prescriber's journey elevates the value of a HIT platform for marketers.

A stronger rapport is built when platforms supply these solutions to ensure a trusted environment is generated to improve the patient's health. The emphasis on quality of care affords platforms an elevated reputation in the category and is viewed highly as a resource at the point-of-care.

When operated properly, sell-side organizations can support providers to improve a patient's health results. The EHR category will transform the space and platforms will continue to advance the communication offerings within EHR systems to be a consistent resource and have a beneficial impact on the treatment a patient receives. With the evolution of EHRs, platforms can formulate online messaging campaign offerings in those digital systems that efficiently unify communications with clinicians that align with the needs of the HCP's digital workflow.

23

ELEVATE eRX POINT-OF-CARE MESSAGING OFFERINGS

Marketers are tasked to reach providers and deliver materials that are hyper-relevant to the prescription that's being written for their patients. The high-impact moment of point-of-care messages emboldens communications to boost script lift when the timing and formats of messages are deployed at the prescribing stage of the HCP's journey.

The proficiency to serve messages following the diagnosis of a patient's condition when the script is being written is a crucial moment for sell-side companies.

To set the foundation for real-time campaigns to be deployed within an eRx channel provides accessibility to the moments when messages about treatment options are top-of-mind as the physician proceeds with advising their patients on therapy.

Generate awareness when a prescription is written

When arriving at the therapy forum of the workflow, platforms can elevate the awareness of prescriptions that are appropriate to treat the patient and enrich the provider-patient dialogue. Hence, platforms must have the ad formats that are suitable to efficiently deliver messages to providers that evoke treatment options that fit the medical needs of a patient.

An example eRx message that was served to a caregiver

When platforms align the deployment of interactions that associate with the stage of care with the patient, the contextual relevance of communications at the prescribing stage of a consultation becomes a powerful asset. The knowledge shared on eRx platforms elevates the HCP-patient relationship as exchanges are distributed to enable educational materials to be shared with a patient via their prescriber.

Educational moments are valuable for communication offerings

Medication adherence can be heavily impacted during interactions that are facilitated within eRx channels. Therefore, the usefulness of a platform that cultivates campaigns in a manner that encourages dialogue about therapies being prescribed is invaluable for life sciences organizations. When messages are served at this point of the provider's journey, the worth of the campaign is enhanced with the ability to raise script lift via the distribution of the campaign.

> The ability to smoothly present messaging opportunities to providers as a prescription is being contemplated can significantly increase the value of an ad slot.

Platforms have the ability to build ad formats that can impact the patient assistance that's available to support a person's adherence to the prescribed therapy. When the eRx is structured to seamlessly inform clinicians about medications, discussions can be held between caregivers and their patients about the monetary cost of a drug, and if it's a viable treatment option for the person.

The aptitude to progress exchanges while drug information is being assessed, prescription coverage is being viewed or a patient's medication fill history is being examined empowers supply-side companies to offer marketers a channel to interact with HCPs when their mindset is focused on treatment options. The distribution of informative messages about therapies at this opportune moment provides an incredible value to reaching a clinician to enhance the health outcomes of their patient.

A platform may be reluctant to introduce ad slots on an eRx medium. However, the capacity to enrich the treatment outcomes by supplying communications that are relevant to the therapy being advised to a patient enables platforms to have a pivotal role in the digital care space. The proficiency to deliver communications within an eRx channel allows platforms to increase the quality of messages that are served at the treatment juncture of the virtual care visit.

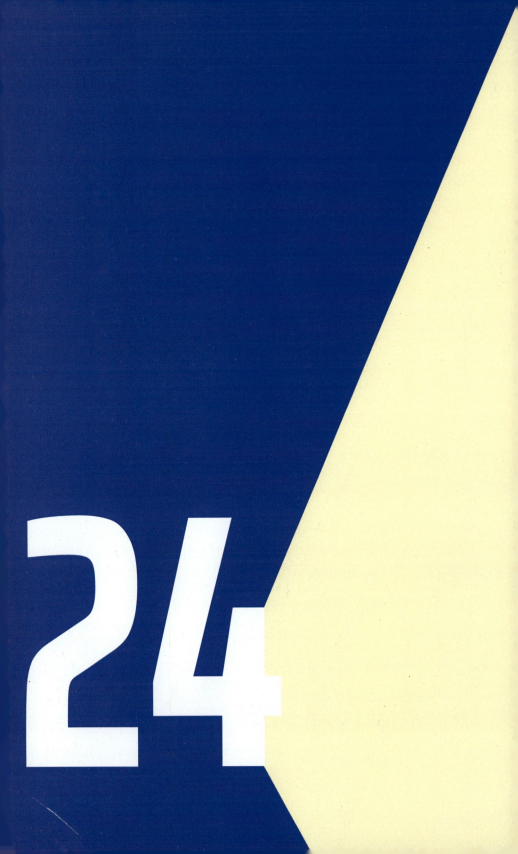

OPTIMIZE INVENTORY OFFERINGS TO BOOST REVENUE

Ad spending on display was the fastest-growing format in the pharma and healthcare sector in 2020. During that year, display ad spending rose by 15.7%, which accounted for $4.04 billion.[97] The demand for effective inventory offerings presents a gainful opportunity for platforms to advance communications in the life sciences industry while generating an additional revenue stream.

In addition, the progression of digital point-of-care campaigns positions platforms to deliver better patient health outcomes. The suppliers of messages to HCPs can enhance the category to ensure educational resources reach providers within online systems while conversing with a patient.

Monetize inventory during the provider's online workflow

During the process of executing communication initiatives at the POC, online solutions will uplift the ability to monetize the inventory of platforms. With the collection of data analytics that further illustrates the virtual workflow of HCPs, the way suppliers structure the formats for campaigns will allow for efficient communications.

Further, the platforms that implement AI-powered platforms can gain actionable insights on the worth of their inventory to maximize the value of ad slots to ensure the revenue being allotted per segment of the medium is reflected accurately in the cost to execute a messaging campaign.

By implementing offerings based on data-driven learnings, the sell-side businesses can facilitate high-quality interactions for life sciences organizations at the point-of-care. Thus, the findings from data analytics collected can showcase the way prescribers are utilizing point-of-care networks to enrich the offerings within a platform.

When evolving the way content is being shared at the point-of-care, the insertion of ad slots within the online channels enables platforms to gain a passive revenue stream. Additionally, programmatic messaging offerings can enrich the treatment environment that is cultivated for clinicians. The passive income enables platforms to increase the company's bottom line with an efficient approach that drives business outcomes across the point-of-care ecosystem.

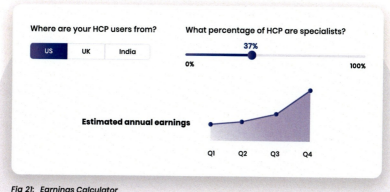

Fig 21: Earnings Calculator

The untapped cash flow opens another way for companies to monetize their business. With the use of data analytics and AI, platforms can identify the key communication offerings within online channels to optimize inventory rates. Programmatic solutions in the space will continue to usher in more real-time insights that can advance the offerings from the sell-side to adjust to the current workflows of prescribers. The moments at the POC and messaging formats that garner greater financial returns for companies then empower platforms to increase bid prices to achieve a higher ROI.

By creating valuable instances for precision messaging within digital channels, platforms can foster more meaningful interactions for life sciences brands with clinicians. Connections with HCPs within point-of-care networks are influential moments that marketers can benefit from to establish a formidable relationship with providers.

With a comprehensive understanding of the sought-after messages that marketers want to share with HCPs, platforms can employ communication offering that enables organizations to reach their coveted providers at the point-of-care.

References

1. Ethan Cramer-Flood. "US Digital Ad Spending by Industry 2021." EMarketer, September 16, 2021. https://www.emarketer.com/content/us-digital-ad-spending-by-industry-2021.0

2. Blake Droesch. "US Healthcare and Pharma Is Among the Fastest-Growing Digital Ad Spenders." EMarketer, October 9, 2020. https://www.emarketer.com/content/us-healthcare-pharma-digital-ad-spending-outlook.

3. Sara Lebow. "US B2B Tech Ad Spending Increased by 50% in 2020." EMarketer, September 10, 2021. https://www.emarketer.com/content/us-b2b-tech-ad-spending-increased-by-50-2020.

4. Robertson, S. L., Robinson, M. D., & Reid, A. (2017). Electronic Health Record Effects on Work-Life Balance and Burnout Within the I3Population Collaborative. Journal of graduate medical education, 9(4), 479–484. https://doi.org/10.4300/JGME-D-16-00123.1

5. Robertson, S. L., Robinson, M. D., & Reid, A. (2017). Electronic Health Record Effects on Work-Life Balance and Burnout Within the I3Population Collaborative. Journal of graduate medical education, 9(4), 479–484. https://doi.org/10.4300/JGME-D-16-00123.1

6. Robertson, S. L., Robinson, M. D., & Reid, A. (2017). Electronic Health Record Effects on Work-Life Balance and Burnout Within the I3Population Collaborative. Journal of graduate medical education, 9(4), 479–484. https://doi.org/10.4300/JGME-D-16-00123.1

7. Oleg Bestsennyy, Greg Gilbert, Alex Harris, and Jennifer Rost. "Telehealth: A Quarter-Trillion-Dollar Post-COVID-19 Reality?," July 9, 2021. https://www.mckinsey.com/industries/healthcare-systems-and-services/our-insights/telehealth-a-quarter-trillion-dollar-post-covid-19-reality.

8. Hannah Nelson. "Google: 9 in 10 Docs Say Interoperability, Data Exchange Top Priority." EHRIntelligence, July 20, 2021. https://ehrintelligence.com/news/google-9-in-10-docs-say-interoperability-data-exchange-top-priority.

9. Brian Schilling. "The Federal Government Has Put Billions into Promoting Electronic Health Record Use: How Is It Going?," n.d. https://www.commonwealthfund.org/publications/newsletter-article/federal-government-has-put-billions-promoting-electronic-health.

10. Reisman M. (2017). EHRs: The Challenge of Making Electronic Data Usable and Interoperable. P & T : a peer-reviewed journal for formulary management, 42(9), 572–575.

11. Hinrichs, S. H., & Zarcone, P. (2013). The Affordable Care Act, meaningful use, and their impact on public health laboratories. Public health reports (Washington, D.C. : 1974), 128 Suppl 2(Suppl 2), 7–9. https://doi.org/10.1177/00333549131280S202

12. Chris Ingersoll. "Moving Beyond EHRs: What Lies Ahead for Healthcare Digitization?" HIT Consultant, July 12, 2021. https://hitconsultant.net/2021/07/12/moving-beyond-ehrs-healthcare-digitization/#.YfRgNi9h1R2.

13. "Certified E-Prescribers Continue to Use Handwritten Scripts," June 4, 2014. https://www.prnewswire.com/news-releases/certified-e-prescribers-continue-to-use-handwritten-scripts-261834541.html.

14. "Surescripts Reports More Than Half of All Prescriptions Routed Electronically in 2013, Driving Adoption of Broader Health Information Exchange," May 22, 2014. https://www.businesswire.com/news/home/20140521005337/en/CORRECTING-and-REPLACING-Surescripts-Reports-More-Than-Half-of-All-Prescriptions-Routed-Electronically-in-2013-Driving-Adoption-of-Broader-Health-Information-Exchange.

15. Surescripts. "2020 National Progress Report," n.d. https://surescripts.com/news-center/national-progress-report-2020.

16. "Outcome Health Agrees to Pay $70 Million to Resolve Fraud Investigation," October 30, 2019. https://www.justice.gov/opa/pr/outcome-health-agrees-pay-70-million-resolve-fraud-investigation.

17. "Outcome Health Agrees to Pay $70 Million to Resolve Fraud Investigation," October 30, 2019. https://www.justice.gov/opa/pr/outcome-health-agrees-pay-70-million-resolve-fraud-investigation.

18. "FTC Charges Surescripts with Illegal Monopolization of E-Prescription Markets," April 24, 2019. https://www.ftc.gov/news-events/news/press-releases/2019/04/ftc-charges-surescripts-illegal-monopolization-e-prescription-markets.

19. Joseph Conn. "Hospitals Achieve 96% EHR Adoption Rate; Data Exchange Still Needs Work," May 31, 2016. https://www.modernhealthcare.com/article/20160531/NEWS/160539990/hospitals-achieve-96-ehr-adoption-rate-data-exchange-still-needs-work.

20. Oleg Bestsennyy, Greg Gilbert, Alex Harris, and Jennifer Rost. "Telehealth: A Quarter-Trillion-Dollar Post-COVID-19 Reality?," July 9, 2021. https://www.mckinsey.com/industries/healthcare-systems-and-services/our-insights/telehealth-a-quarter-trillion-dollar-post-covid-19-reality.

21. Surescripts. "2020 National Progress Report," n.d. https://surescripts.com/news-center/national-progress-report-2020.

22. Kaiser Family Foundation. "2019 Employer Health Benefits Survey," September 25, 2019. https://www.kff.org/report-section/ehbs-2019-section-14-employer-practices-and-health-plan-networks/#figure145.

23. Kaiser Family Foundation. "2019 Employer Health Benefits Survey," September 25, 2019. https://www.kff.org/report-section/ehbs-2019-section-14-employer-practices-and-health-plan-networks/#figure145.

24. Oleg Bestsennyy, Greg Gilbert, Alex Harris, and Jennifer Rost. "Telehealth: A Quarter-Trillion-Dollar Post-COVID-19 Reality?," July 9, 2021. https://www.mckinsey.com/industries/healthcare-systems-and-services/our-insights/telehealth-a-quarter-trillion-dollar-post-covid-19-reality.

25. Rebecca Pifer. "Telehealth Use Stabilizing at 38 Times Pre-COVID-19 Levels, McKinsey Says." Healthcare Dive, July 12, 2021. https://www.healthcaredive.com/news/telehealth-use-stabilizing-at-38-times-pre-covid-19-levels-mckinsey-says/603153/.

26. Dan Witters. "In U.S., an Estimated 18 Million Can't Pay for Needed Drugs," n.d. https://news.gallup.com/poll/354833/estimated-million-pay-needed-drugs.aspx.

27. Veradigm. "How Can Improved Medication Adherence Promote Value-Based Care?," n.d. https://www.mmm-online.com/home/channel/sponsored/how-can-improved-medication-adherence-promote-value-based-care/.

28. Peter Adams. "Data Marketing Spend Tops $29B in US as Cookie Deadline Looms." Marketing Dive, January 24, 2022. https://www.marketingdive.com/news/data-marketing-spend-tops-29b-in-us-as-cookie-deadline-looms/617539/.

29. Peter Adams. "Data Marketing Spend Tops $29B in US as Cookie Deadline Looms." Marketing Dive, January 24, 2022. https://www.marketingdive.com/news/data-marketing-spend-tops-29b-in-us-as-cookie-deadline-looms/617539/.

30. Julian Upton. "AI and Analytics Appear Ready to Surge in Sales and Marketing." Pharmaceutical Executive, February 9, 2022. https://www.pharmexec.com/view/ai-and-analytics-appear-ready-to-surge-in-sales-and-marketing.

31. "Gartner Says 63% of Digital Marketing Leaders Still Struggle with Personalization, Yet Only 17% Use AI and Machine Learning Across the Function," n.d. https://www.gartner.com/en/newsroom/press-releases/-gartner-says-63--of-digital-marketing-leaders-still-struggle-wi.

32. "Electronic Health Records Market Size, Share & Trends Analysis Report," n.d. https://www.grandviewresearch.com/industry-analysis/electronic-health-records-ehr-market.

33. Liang, J., Li, Y., Zhang, Z., Shen, D., Xu, J., Zheng, X., Wang, T., Tang, B., Lei, J., & Zhang, J. (2021). Adoption of Electronic Health Records (EHRs) in China During the Past 10 Years: Consecutive Survey Data Analysis and Comparison of Sino-American Challenges and Experiences. Journal of medical Internet research, 23(2), e24813. https://doi.org/10.2196/24813

34. Liang, J., Li, Y., Zhang, Z., Shen, D., Xu, J., Zheng, X., Wang, T., Tang, B., Lei, J., & Zhang, J. (2021). Adoption of Electronic Health Records (EHRs) in China During the Past 10 Years: Consecutive Survey Data Analysis and Comparison of Sino-American Challenges and Experiences. Journal of medical Internet research, 23(2), e24813. https://doi.org/10.2196/24813

35. Liang, J., Li, Y., Zhang, Z., Shen, D., Xu, J., Zheng, X., Wang, T., Tang, B., Lei, J., & Zhang, J. (2021). Adoption of Electronic Health Records (EHRs) in China During the Past 10 Years: Consecutive Survey Data Analysis and Comparison of Sino-American Challenges and Experiences. Journal of medical Internet research, 23(2), e24813. https://doi.org/10.2196/24813

36. Mike Miliard. "Epic, Cerner, Allscripts Gaining Traction in a European EHR Market That's in Competitive Flux." Healthcare IT News, August 28, 2018. https://www.healthcareitnews.com/news/epic-cerner-allscripts-gaining-traction-european-ehr-market-thats-competitive-flux.

37. Mallory Hackett. "The Digital Transformation in Healthcare Has Just Begun, According to Accenture Report." MobiHealthNews, June 21, 2021. https://www.mobihealthnews.com/news/digital-transformation-healthcare-has-just-begun-according-accenture-report.

38. Lecia Bushak. "Pharma Content for HCPs: Better, but with Room for Improvement." MM+M, December 14, 2021. https://www.mmm-online.com/home/channel/pharma-content-for-hcps-better-but-with-room-for-improvement/.

39. Lecia Bushak. "Pharma Content for HCPs: Better, but with Room for Improvement." MM+M, December 14, 2021. https://www.mmm-online.com/home/channel/pharma-content-for-hcps-better-but-with-room-for-improvement/.

40. Matt Hollingsworth and Andrew Shin. "The Growing Issue of Healthcare Provider Burnout: Can AI Help?" MedCity News, January 28, 2022. https://medcitynews.com/2022/01/the-growing-issue-of-healthcare-provider-burnout-can-ai-help/.

41. Matt Hollingsworth and Andrew Shin. "The Growing Issue of Healthcare Provider Burnout: Can AI Help?" MedCity News, January 28, 2022. https://medcitynews.com/2022/01/the-growing-issue-of-healthcare-provider-burnout-can-ai-help/.

42. Rebecca Pifer. "Hospital Telehealth Leveling off at One-Fifth of Medical Appointments, Research Finds." Healthcare Dive, September 7, 2021. https://www.healthcaredive.com/news/hospital-telehealth-leveling-off-at-one-fifth-of-medical-appointments-rese/606126/.

43. Anuja Vaidya. "55% of Telehealth Providers Frustrated With Overblown Patient Expectations." MHealth Intelligence, March 18, 2022. https://mhealthintelligence.com/news/55-of-telehealth-providers-frustrated-with-overblown-patient-expectations.

44. DocASAP. "Provider Telehealth Use and Experience Survey," n.d. https://indd.adobe.com/view/f2fb8b7-98e7-459a-9975-82aeb274c928.

45. Rebecca Pifer. "Telehealth Use Stabilizing at 38 Times Pre-COVID-19 Levels, McKinsey Says." Healthcare Dive, July 12, 2021. https://www.healthcaredive.com/news/telehealth-use-stabilizing-at-38-times-pre-covid-19-levels-mckinsey-says/603153/.

46. John Commins. "National Survey Gives Telehealth Good Reviews." HealthLeaders, August 10, 2021. https://www.healthleadersmedia.com/telehealth/national-survey-gives-telehealth-good-reviews.

47. "Where Did US Telehealth Users Receive Their Follow-Up Care After the Initial Telehealth Service?," April 11, 2021. https://www.emarketer.com/chart/246450/where-us-telehealth-users-receive-their-follow-up-care-after-initial-telehealth-service-of-respondents-feb-2021.

48. Mike Miliard. "Telehealth Has Grown by Leaps at Doc Practices, with Wide Variance in Usage Patterns." Healthcare IT News, September 15, 2021. https://www.healthcareitnews.com/news/telehealth-has-grown-leaps-doc-practices-wide-variance-usage-patterns.

49. Lecia Bushak. "Telehealth Usage Drops among Certain Specialties, Survey Shows." MM+M, March 15, 2022. https://www.mmm-online.com/home/channel/telehealth-usage-drops-among-certain-specialties-survey-shows/.

50. Emma Bardin. "Global Survey: More than Half of Clinicians Say Telehealth Harms Their Ability to Show Empathy towards Patients." MedCity News, March 15, 2022. https://medcitynews.com/2022/03/global-survey-more-than-half-of-clinicians-say-telehealth-harms-their-ability-to-show-empathy-towards-patients/.

51. Paige Minemyer. "Optum Survey: Providers See Telehealth as Convenient, but Frustrations Remain." Fierce Healthcare, March 15, 2022. https://www.fiercehealthcare.com/telehealth/optum-survey-providers-see-telehealth-convenient-frustrations-remain.

52. "What Is the HITECH Act?," n.d. https://www.hipaajournal.com/what-is-the-hitech-act/.

53. Reisman M. (2017). EHRs: The Challenge of Making Electronic Data Usable and Interoperable. P & T : a peer-reviewed journal for formulary management, 42(9), 572–575.

54. Joanne Finnegan. "For Each Patient Visit, Physicians Spend about 16 Minutes on EHRs, Study Finds." Fierce Healthcare, January 14, 2020. https://www.fiercehealthcare.com/practices/for-each-patient-visit-physicians-spend-about-16-minutes-ehrs-study-finds.

55. Joanne Finnegan. "For Each Patient Visit, Physicians Spend about 16 Minutes on EHRs, Study Finds." Fierce Healthcare, January 14, 2020. https://www.fiercehealthcare.com/practices/for-each-patient-visit-physicians-spend-about-16-minutes-ehrs-study-finds.

56. Dr. John Ciccone. "Bringing the Human Element Back to Healthcare." MedCity News, December 2, 2021. https://medcitynews.com/2021/12/bringing-the-human-element-back-to-healthcare/.

57. Joanne Finnegan. "For Each Patient Visit, Physicians Spend about 16 Minutes on EHRs, Study Finds." Fierce Healthcare, January 14, 2020. https://www.fiercehealthcare.com/practices/for-each-patient-visit-physicians-spend-about-16-minutes-ehrs-study-finds.

58. Hannah Nelson. "Google: 9 in 10 Docs Say Interoperability, Data Exchange Top Priority." EHRIntelligence, July 20, 2021. https://ehrintelligence.com/news/google-9-in-10-docs-say-interoperability-data-exchange-top-priority.

59. Hannah Nelson. "Google: 9 in 10 Docs Say Interoperability, Data Exchange Top Priority." EHRIntelligence, July 20, 2021. https://ehrintelligence.com/news/google-9-in-10-docs-say-interoperability-data-exchange-top-priority.

60. Veradigm. "6 Questions You Should Be Asking Your Digital Point-of-Care Media Vendor." MM+M, April 13, 2021. https://www.mmm-online.com/home/channel/sponsored/6-questions-you-should-be-asking-your-digital-point-of-care-media-vendor/.

61. Doug Bonderud. "EMRs vs. EHRs: What's the Difference?" HealthTech, July 29, 2021. https://healthtechmagazine.net/article/2021/07/emrs-vs-ehrs-whats-difference-perfcon.

62. Katie Adams. "31 Numbers That Show How Big Epic, Cerner, Allscripts & Meditech Are in Healthcare." Becker's Health IT, April 12, 2021. https://www.beckershospitalreview.com/healthcare-information-technology/31-numbers-that-show-how-big-epic-cerner-allscripts-meditech-are-in-healthcare.html.

63. Katie Adams. "31 Numbers That Show How Big Epic, Cerner, Allscripts & Meditech Are in Healthcare." Becker's Health IT, April 12, 2021. https://www.beckershospitalreview.com/healthcare-information-technology/31-numbers-that-show-how-big-epic-cerner-allscripts-meditech-are-in-healthcare.html.

64. Jeff Green. "Who Are the Largest EHR Vendors." EHR in Practice, November 12, 2021. https://www.ehrinpractice.com/largest-ehr-vendors.html.

65. Jeff Green. "Who Are the Largest EHR Vendors." EHR in Practice, November 12, 2021. https://www.ehrinpractice.com/largest-ehr-vendors.html.

66. Christopher Jason. "COVID-19 Triggers Increase in EPrescribing, Interoperability Tools." EHRIntelligence, April 20, 2021. https://ehrintelligence.com/news/covid-19-triggers-increase-in-eprescribing-interoperability-tools.

67. Hannah Nelson. "Surescripts Report Reveals 2021 Health IT Interoperability Gains." EHRIntelligence, March 15, 2022. https://ehrintelligence.com/news/surescripts-report-reveals-2021-health-it-interoperability-gains.

68. Surescripts. "2021 National Progress Report," n.d. https://surescripts.com/docs/default-source/national-progress-reports/2021-national-progress-report.pdf?sfvrsn=71fcbe15_12.

69. Surescripts. "2021 National Progress Report," n.d. https://surescripts.com/docs/default-source/national-progress-reports/2021-national-progress-report.pdf?sfvrsn=71fcbe15_12.

70. Robert Langreth. "Drug Prices." Bloomberg, September 16, 2020. https://www.bloomberg.com/quicktake/drug-prices.

71. Beth Snyder Bulik. "Pharmas' Return on $5B Spent Yearly on Patient Support Programs? Only 3% Are Using Them: Survey." Fierce Pharma, July 6, 2021. https://www.fiercepharma.com/marketing/pharmas-return-5-billion-spent-yearly-patient-support-programs-only-3-use-survey.

72. Beth Snyder Bulik. "Pharmas' Return on $5B Spent Yearly on Patient Support Programs? Only 3% Are Using Them: Survey." Fierce Pharma, July 6, 2021. https://www.fiercepharma.com/marketing/pharmas-return-5-billion-spent-yearly-patient-support-programs-only-3-use-survey.

73. Beth Snyder Bulik. "Pharmas' Return on $5B Spent Yearly on Patient Support Programs? Only 3% Are Using Them: Survey." Fierce Pharma, July 6, 2021. https://www.fiercepharma.com/marketing/pharmas-return-5-billion-spent-yearly-patient-support-programs-only-3-use-survey.

74. Sanjay K. Rao, PhD. "How Medication Non-Adherence Impacts Brand Management." Pharmaceutical Executive, March 24, 2021. https://www.pharmexec.com/view/how-medication-non-adherence-impacts-brand-management.

75. Eric Wicklund. "Digital Health Tech, New Strategies Improve Medication Management." HealthLeaders, March 29, 2022. https://www.healthleadersmedia.com/innovation/digital-health-tech-new-strategies-improve-medication-management.

76. Lecia Bushak. "4 Takeaways from Accenture's Healthcare Experience Survey." MM+M, August 25, 2021. https://www.mmm-online.com/home/channel/4-takeaways-from-accentures-healthcare-experience-survey/.

77. Dan Witters. "In U.S., an Estimated 18 Million Can't Pay for Needed Drugs," September 21, 2021. https://news.gallup.com/poll/354835/estimated-million-pay-needed-drugs.aspx.

78. Sara Heath. "Patient-Provider Communication Misses the Mark on Medication Adherence." PatientEngagementHIT, November 30, 2021. https://patientengagementhit.com/news/patient-provider-communication-misses-the-mark-on-medication-adherence.

79. Sara Heath. "Patient-Provider Communication Misses the Mark on Medication Adherence." PatientEngagementHIT, November 30, 2021. https://patientengagementhit.com/news/patient-provider-communication-misses-the-mark-on-medication-adherence.

80. Mallory Hackett. "The Digital Transformation in Healthcare Has Just Begun, According to Accenture Report." MobiHealthNews, June 21, 2021. https://www.mobihealthnews.com/news/digital-transformation-healthcare-has-just-begun-according-accenture-report.

81. Robert Williams. "Gartner: 63% of Marketers Struggle with Personalization Tech." Marketing Dive, April 15, 2021. https://www.marketingdive.com/news/gartner-63-of-marketers-struggle-with-personalization-tech/598433/.

82. Robert Williams. "Gartner: 63% of Marketers Struggle with Personalization Tech." Marketing Dive, April 15, 2021. https://www.marketingdive.com/news/gartner-63-of-marketers-struggle-with-personalization-tech/598433/.

83. Sameer Khanna. "The Value of a Human-Centric, AI-Powered Approach to Healthcare." MedCity News, February 27, 2022. https://medcitynews.com/2022/02/the-value-of-a-human-centric-ai-powered-approach-to-healthcare/.

84. Bohr, A., & Memarzadeh, K. (2020). The rise of artificial intelligence in healthcare applications. Artificial Intelligence in Healthcare, 25–60. https://doi.org/10.1016/B978-0-12-818438-7.00002-2

85. Rebecca Torrence. "Providers Still Skeptical about Wearable Accuracy, Integration Abilities." Fierce Healthcare, December 6, 2021. https://www.fiercehealthcare.com/tech/providers-still-skeptical-about-wearable-accuracy-integration-abilities.

86. Accenture. "Is COVID-19 Altering How Pharma Engages with HCPs?," August 4, 2021. https://www.accenture.com/us-en/insights/life-sciences/coronavirus-changing-pharma-hcp-engagement.

87. Anuja Vaidya. "51% of Clinicians Worry That Telehealth Hinders Ability to Show Empathy." MHealth Intelligence, March 15, 2022. https://mhealthintelligence.com/news/51-of-clinicians-worry-that-telehealth-hinders-ability-to-show-empathy.

88. Scott Mace. "Healthcare Leaders Identify Top Digital Transformation Priorities for Healthcare." HealthLeaders, July 26, 2021. https://www.healthleadersmedia.com/technology/healthcare-leaders-identify-top-digital-transformation-priorities-healthcare.

89. Ben Adams. "The Drive to Digital in Pharma Marketing Is 'overwhelming' Doctors. Solution? Train Digitally Savvy Reps." Fierce Pharma, January 10, 2022. https://www.fiercepharma.com/marketing/drive-to-digital-pharma-marketing-overwhelming-doctors-as-industry-must-train-up.

90. Ben Adams. "The Drive to Digital in Pharma Marketing Is 'overwhelming' Doctors. Solution? Train Digitally Savvy Reps." Fierce Pharma, January 10, 2022. https://www.fiercepharma.com/marketing/drive-to-digital-pharma-marketing-overwhelming-doctors-as-industry-must-train-up.

91. Scott Mace. "Healthcare Leaders Identify Top Digital Transformation Priorities for Healthcare." HealthLeaders, July 26, 2021. https://www.healthleadersmedia.com/technology/healthcare-leaders-identify-top-digital-transformation-priorities-healthcare.

92. Kat Jercich. "Telehealth Revenue Could Hit $20B in Five Years, Say Analysts." Healthcare IT News, February 25, 2022. https://www.healthcareitnews.com/news/telehealth-revenue-could-hit-20b-five-years-say-analysts.

93. Jeff Lagasse. "Telehealth Will Endure, but Providers Are Managing Expectations." Healthcare Finance, March 22, 2022. https://www.healthcarefinancenews.com/news/telehealth-will-endure-providers-are-managing-expectations.

94. Jeff Lagasse. "Telehealth Will Endure, but Providers Are Managing Expectations." Healthcare Finance, March 22, 2022. https://www.healthcarefinancenews.com/news/telehealth-will-endure-providers-are-managing-expectations.

95. Jeff Lagasse. "Telehealth Will Endure, but Providers Are Managing Expectations." Healthcare Finance, March 22, 2022. https://www.healthcarefinancenews.com/news/telehealth-will-endure-providers-are-managing-expectations.

96. Erin McNemar, MPA. "Artificial Intelligence Assists with EHR Data Organization." HealthITAnalytics, July 27, 2021. https://healthitanalytics.com/news/artificial-intelligence-assists-with-ehr-data-organization.

97. Blake Droesch. "US Healthcare and Pharma Digital Ad Spending 2020." EMarketer, September 30, 2022. https://www.emarketer.com/content/us-healthcare-pharma-digital-ad-spending-2020.

List of Figures

1. Blake Droesch. "US Healthcare and Pharma Is Among the Fastest-Growing Digital Ad Spenders." EMarketer, October 9, 2020. https://www.emarketer.com/content/us-healthcare-pharma-digital-ad-spending-outlook.

2. Surescripts. "2020 National Progress Report," n.d. https://surescripts.com/news-center/national-progress-report-2020.

3. Oleg Bestsennyy, Greg Gilbert, Alex Harris, and Jennifer Rost. "Telehealth: A Quarter-Trillion-Dollar Post-COVID-19 Reality?," July 9, 2021. https://www.mckinsey.com/industries/healthcare-systems-and-services/our-insights/telehealth-a-quarter-trillion-dollar-post-covid-19-reality.

4. "Epic App Orchard Explore Apps," n.d. https://apporchard.epic.com/Gallery?contexts=100.

5. "Cerner Open Developer Experience App Gallery," n.d. https://code.cerner.com/apps.

6. "What Is the HITECH Act?," n.d. https://www.hipaajournal.com/what-is-the-hitech-act/.

7. Surescripts. "2021 National Progress Report," n.d. https://surescripts.com/docs/default-source/national-progress-reports/2021-national-progress-report.pdf?sfvrsn=71fcbe15_12.

8. "Electronic Health Records Market Size, Share & Trends Analysis Report," n.d. https://www.grandviewresearch.com/industry-analysis/electronic-health-records-ehr-market.

9. Vikram Kapur, Satyam Mehra, Alex Boulton, and Lucy d'Arville. "Asia-Pacific Front Line of Healthcare Report 2022," January 14, 2022. https://www.bain.com/insights/asia-pacific-front-line-of-healthcare-report-2022/.

10. Vikram Kapur, Satyam Mehra, Alex Boulton, and Lucy d'Arville. "Asia-Pacific Front Line of Healthcare Report 2022," January 14, 2022. https://www.bain.com/insights/asia-pacific-front-line-of-healthcare-report-2022/.

11. Sara Lebow. "The Top Ways US Patients Are Using Telehealth." EMarketer, January 18, 2022. https://www.emarketer.com/content/us-patients-telehealth.

12. Paige Minemyer. "Optum Survey: Providers See Telehealth as Convenient, but Frustrations Remain." Fierce Healthcare, March 15, 2022. https://www.fiercehealthcare.com/telehealth/optum-survey-providers-see-telehealth-convenient-frustrations-remain.

13. "Where Did US Telehealth Users Receive Their Follow-Up Care After the Initial Telehealth Service?," April 11, 2021. https://www.emarketer.com/chart/246450/where-us-telehealth-users-receive-their-follow-up-care-after-initial-telehealth-service-of-respondents-feb-2021.

14. "Telemedicine," n.d. https://www.patientclick.com/solutions/telemedicine.aspx.

15. Reisman M. (2017). EHRs: The Challenge of Making Electronic Data Usable and Interoperable. P & T : a peer-reviewed journal for formulary management, 42(9), 572–575.

16. "Cerner Open Developer Experience App Gallery," n.d. https://code.cerner.com/apps; "Epic App Orchard Explore Apps," n.d. https://apporchard.epic.com/Gallery?contexts=100; "Greenway Marketplace," n.d. https://www.greenwayhealth.com/marketplace.

17. Rayna Hollander. "How 5G Will Change Healthcare." EMarketer, March 18, 2021. https://www.emarketer.com/content/how-5g-will-change-healthcare.

18. Rhea Patel. "Why Legacy Medtech Giants Are Swooping into the Digital Health Market." EMarketer, February 24, 2022. https://www.emarketer.com/content/why-legacy-medtech-giants-swooping-digital-health-market.

19. Doceree. "Ad Slot Integration," n.d. https://support.doceree.com/hc/en-us/articles/360063319473-Ad-Slot-integration.

20. Jeff Lagasse. "Telehealth Will Endure, but Providers Are Managing Expectations." Healthcare Finance, March 22, 2022. https://www.healthcarefinancenews.com/news/telehealth-will-endure-providers-are-managing-expectations.

21. Doceree. "Earnings Calculator," n.d. https://doceree.com/publisher/us/earnings-calculator/.